HOODWINKED*

UNCOVERING OUR FUNDAMENTAL SUPERSTITIONS

Larry Gottlieb

(*Hoodwinked: to deceive or trick, to blindfold)

CONTENTS

DEDICATION

for all who hear the whispering...

"For me there is only the traveling on the paths that have heart, on any path that may have a heart. There I travel, and the only worthwhile challenge for me is to travel its full length. And there I travel—looking, looking, breathlessly."

—Don Juan Matus
as told to Carlos Castaneda

"It's much easier to ride the horse in the direction he's going."

—Werner Erhard

"Ask and It Is Given."

—Esther Hicks as Abraham

Hoodwinked: To deceive or trick; to blindfold

FOREWORD

...and the Voice said, **"Don't worry Larry; we'll get you home."**

Something happened to me one day in 1974 that would forever change the way I look at life. And I have since found that once you go through that door, you can never go back.

CHAPTER 1

HOW DOES THE WORLD LOOK TO A FISH?

A parable to start us off

Imagine, if you will, that each of us is a newborn fish. In the few days since we were born, we've cautiously swum about some, but now Mom has gathered us together to teach us about our world.

She points out rocks, and that some good things to eat might be found around them. She tells us about the sand, and that there are some creatures that look like sand but might sting us. She lets us know about what's good to eat and what might want to eat us, and eventually we come to feel as if we have this fish thing wired.

What she doesn't tell us about, of course, is water, because she doesn't know about water. She doesn't know about water because water is all she has ever known. But imagine that one day something happens to you that takes you out of your well-understood reality. In this case, it comes in the form of feeling something sharp and foreign in your mouth. You're jerked around and pulled upwards, and suddenly you cross

THE CONVENTIONAL EXPLANATION OF THE WORLD IS NEVER EXAMINED

some sort of boundary and you can't breathe. You've been caught! Fortunately for you, you're in a catch-and-release area and you're gently put back where you belong. And now you know about the existence of water. You know about water by experiencing what we might call 'not-water', so that you can now distinguish water from everything else.

One day many years ago, I found out about the water I'd been swimming in. And that changed everything.

For human beings of course, the water in this parable doesn't represent a physical thing. Instead, it takes the form of an explanation of what we see and hear. It is a conventional understanding we have of the world and of our place in it.

However, like the fish in our parable, we look *through*, and not *at*, this understanding. It is transparent, like the water the fish swims in. We never think about our idea of the world, and for the most part we're not even aware that we have one. It's all we know. And the totality of how we look at ourselves, at life, at the world, our entire belief system, is based on this invisible understanding.

For us humans, this conventional explanation is rooted in one fundamental idea: that the world exists pretty much as we perceive it to be, whether or not we are around to perceive it. It's a natural, intuitive assumption. We all 'know' that when we look at something, we're seeing it more or less the way it actually is.

However, it turns out that there is a completely different interpretation we can make of what we see with our physical eyes. And that understanding leads to a stunningly new vision of what it is to be a human being. Come along with me and we'll discover it together!

CHAPTER 2

HOW DO WE SEE OURSELVES?

The stories we tell

Let me tell you a story. "Wait," you say, "I thought this was a nonfiction book!" It is. Ultimately, all nonfiction is a story. That may be counter-intuitive at first hearing. We tend to think of it as the truth, or as what actually happened. In other words, we think of nonfiction as 'just the facts.'

However, if you look at any book in the nonfiction section of a bookstore or library, you won't find 'just the facts' about anything. You'll find books that reflect the dictionary definition of nonfiction: "narrative prose offering opinions or conjectures upon facts and reality." Delving further, we find that the word narrative refers to "story or account of events whether true or fictitious."

Essentially, all this boils down to nonfiction as story and interpretation. Interpretation includes opinion and conjecture, as well as explanation. Interpretation explains the meaning of things. The oldest part of our human brain is programmed to do that continuously, interpreting everything we perceive in terms of whether we need a response, be it fight or flight, or more generally sensing whether what we are perceiving is of value in terms of survival.

The brain needs a basis on which to interpret perception, and that basis is memory. Memory is the record of the past, whether written or oral. Memory can be thought of as the recording of interpretation. We can look at our memories as a series of multi-sensory images (visual, audible, and so on) of what we have perceived. Those images tell a story, a story in pictures. Any time you're thinking about things, which I bet is most of the time, you're telling yourself stories. These stories explain what you have experienced and what you are likely to experience going forward.

What about when you're not looking at your memories, but instead when you're in the present moment experiencing something right now? In that case, you're processing the information from your senses, and a larger part of your brain is figuring out what that information means. It's interpreting what you see and hear with a much larger scope than fight or flight but built on that same structure. It's telling you a story about what you're perceiving.

I used to study physics. When someone asks me what part of physics I liked most, I tell them "cosmology." Strictly speaking, cosmology is the science of the origin and development of the physical universe, and it's pretty obvious that cosmology is nonfiction. But as we saw, nonfiction is a story, and cosmology is no exception. It's an interpretation of the answers we've gotten as we ask questions like "How did the universe begin?" and "What determined why it came to be the way we observe it to be?" And that story is told in terms of things like big bang, inflation, the expansion of space, and so on.

So, cosmology is an explanation. We human beings have explanations for everything. That seems to be part of what it is to be human. You could even say that humans have a basic hunger for them, for answers, for meanings. I am considering a specific explanation in this work, and it is the one about who we *really* are and what the world out there *really* is. It's my preferred cosmology, so to speak, and it is an alternative cosmology to the one we inherited from our birth culture.

The story I'm telling you in this book is a story about searching for a deeper understanding of what it is to be a human being than the one we carry around with us. It is an account of an inquiry into that understanding based on the only possible raw material upon which such a search could possibly be based, and for me that is my own life experience. Along my way on this path of inquiry, I came to see that our interpretation of what we are perceiving is all we have, and in describing our perceptions we are creating a story. The purpose of the story I am telling in this book is to provide a platform upon which a seeker of truth can stand and look outward for him or herself.

Before I present an alternative explanation, I will first summarize the one all of us already use, the story we tell ourselves, the one into which we live our lives. That story is represented by the water in our fish parable. As I suggested, it is transparent and invisible. But we will see if we can get a feel for it anyway.

How do we think about ourselves?

The metaphorical water we humans swim in consists of many stories with a common thread and a common basis. What is common to all these stories is that there *is* a world, it existed before you and I were around to experience it, and it continues to exist independently of us. In these stories, the world has existed for a length of time measured in billions of years. Once it began, it continued to evolve according to the laws of physics, some of which we have managed to explain to ourselves and others we've not.

After an incredibly long period of time, life appeared on at least one planet, the one we consider the Home Planet. Creatures slowly evolved with the mental and sensory apparatus required to see, hear, feel, taste, and smell the world. And finally, humans appeared, creatures able to experience the world and possessing the cognitive abilities required to think about it, to plan, to analyze, and even to understand.

According to the universally accepted explanation—what I call the water we swim in—what we humans are is first and foremost an enormously complex collection of atoms, atoms that form molecules, molecules that form cells, cells that form tissues, and so on. This progression of collections proceeds according to strict rules, rules which allow for variations and new forms. And somehow, according to this story, out of that enormous complexity arose awareness, thoughts, feelings, and emotions, all the strange and wonderful aspects to 'being human.'

Parallel to that story, there is another set of stories about why we humans are here. Some folks say we are here simply because of the predictable or accidental unfolding of nature's laws, laws which led to our evolution from 'lesser' animals. Others say we are here to work out karma or to pay off karmic debts. Or that we're here to 'fulfill God's purpose.' And for some, there is quite simply a feeling that there may not be any answer to that question about why we are here, other than, perhaps, random accident.

That's the default cosmology, the story about our presence in the world we inherited from our culture. In this book, I'm arguing for the consideration of a different cosmology. This other explanation, this other story we could tell ourselves, is a completely different story about what we are, why we are here, and the purpose of our lives. I call it the 'seer's explanation.' When I use the word 'seer', I'm not referring to seeing auras or energy fields or the future. I'm using it in the sense in which one suddenly recognizes the presence of something that previously had been invisible or just disregarded, as in the phrase 'Ah! I see'! This seer's explanation is a description of human experience which is in sharp contrast to the ordinary explanation.

At this point, a typical rational person would ask, "But is this other story true?" When one argues for or against an explanation from a rational point of view, our most important criterion for evaluating that explanation is whether or not it is true. In this book, I will attempt to show that the word 'true', while useful in describing a particular fact, event, or situation, takes on a completely different meaning when considering an explanation for the world we experience and for our presence in it.

What is a human being, anyway?

With that background, let's return to the question, 'What is a human being?' In terms of the prevailing secular story, the term 'human being' refers to a template handed down by the process of evolution and encoded in our DNA. Starting with that template, the differences among us are accounted for by appeals to 'nature' and 'nurture.' These terms, of course, refer to circumstances of birth, in which genetic, societal, and environmental factors give us different combinations of attributes and paths through life. We should, of course, also include the results of decisions we make, using our free will, about what we should have, or do, or become.

Ultimately, according to the prevailing cosmology, we humans are transients here on a planet that happens to be revolving at just the right distance from an ordinary star so as to provide the particular combination of heat, light, and the substances required to sustain the chemical processes necessary for life as we know it.

We've probably all encountered the pseudo-philosophical question, 'If a tree falls in the forest, and there's no one around to hear, will it still make a sound?' An equivalent question relevant to our topic is, 'If all sentient creatures somehow disappeared, would there still be a planet, revolving through space and time around a star?' According to the universally accepted explanation, there is no need to ask that question. We are certain that there would be a planet if we all disappeared.

But what if that which we think of as the entire physical universe is actually a story? What if it is actually *a description, an interpretation of what we see, a set of ideas about the world?* In that case, it is not at all clear that such a story can exist without the human being that's doing the storytelling.

If you accept the default cosmology, the story we all came to 'swim' in, it seems to me that human awareness and consciousness must somehow be a byproduct of natural forces and processes. Now, if that's your explanation for the appearance of consciousness in the universe, I think your stance begs a few remarkably interesting questions. Is it just a happy accident, a product of a particularly fortunate assembling of the elements of our physical world, that physics and chemistry should give rise to biology and consciousness? Can molecular biology possibly explain the richness of human experience, the depth of feelings, or the pull of abstract ideas? Can it possibly explain love? And finally, does that explanation really satisfy anyone? It certainly never satisfied me.

CHAPTER 3

EARLY WHISPERINGS

My first look at physics

In high school, I discovered that I was 'turned on' by physics. It was in those classes that I first felt the beginnings of my own intellectual fire. The topics were basic, mostly classical mechanics and electromagnetism, and the lab equipment was rudimentary by today's standards, but still it sparked my interest. I recall feeling excited when I grasped some concept the teacher was explaining. That excitement was a hint of what would later become the central passion of my life's work.

Later, continuing my study of physics at M.I.T., I wrote a paper in which another, somewhat more developed hint appears. I expressed the idea that we can never know what something is, but only what it does, or how it behaves. For example, I argued that objects *reflect* light in a certain way, light which then enters our eyes and creates electrical signals. These signals travel to our brains, which then create the experience of vision. I also pointed out that the electrons in the object's atoms *interact* with those in our skin to provide, through the physics of electrostatics, the experience of touch. Those verbs 'reflect' and 'interact' indicate that the object in question behaves in a certain way when we encounter it. Even then, it seemed to me that, equipped with only our five senses, we cannot know what something really is but only how it interacts with us. This idea became central to my current thesis, as we shall see.

My first look at philosophy

During my undergraduate years, I studied traditional philosophy and its practitioners' attempts to explain what human beings can know. This inquiry is what philosophers call epistemology. I read Aristotle, writing in the 4th century BCE, and Kant, in the 18th century CE. I studied David Hume, also of the 18th century, who argued that "humans have knowledge only of things they directly experience." I read Bishop George Berkeley, who in the early 18th century advanced a theory he called 'immaterialism.' This theory, according to Wikipedia, "denies the existence of material substance and instead contends that familiar objects like tables and chairs are ideas perceived by the minds and, as a result, cannot exist without being perceived." At the time, these ideas were, almost in equal measure, interesting and baffling to me. As we shall see, however, Berkeley anticipated a key principle of quantum theory by about two hundred years.

I studied physics throughout my undergraduate years and for about a year and a half of graduate school. As I recall, the material was presented largely in its rigorous mathematical formulation, with only occasional conversations about the underlying abstractions and meaning, what is 'actually' going on. When I thought about a career in physics, it seemed it would most likely be as a professor, but those thoughts did not ignite real lasting passion in me. In retrospect, I see that I was being given a hint as to how best to use this training in physics: as a guide to visualization and not as a rigorous discipline.

My first look at politics

In 1969, while still in graduate school, my pursuit of understanding and knowledge was redirected. I became drawn in by the opposition among my fellow students to the war in Vietnam. In addition to my feelings about the war itself, I began to be concerned with the political and economic factors that appeared to cause a great deal of human suffering both at home and abroad. Those concerns were consistent with values I had learned at home. I joined with others to publish an 'underground' newspaper through which we could express these ideas.

As opposition to the war (and to the 'power structure' that appeared to support it) increased, so did the pushback on the part of those who were apparently committed to the status quo and who seemed to feel threatened by our activities. The pushback escalated into bullet holes in our office door, break-ins and destruction of essential equipment, and finally the firebombing of my car. That was enough for me. I had been given a glimpse of what I now see as the futility of resistance to what is, and I fled to the next chapter in my life. I had played rock guitar in college, and when a friend invited me to come to Aspen to play a few gigs, it seemed like the obvious thing to do.

My first look at living authentically

Moving full-time to Aspen, Colorado, in the fall of 1970, I discovered there a musical community in which I felt at home in a way I never had before. The feelings I had then were summarized for me a few years later, when John Denver wrote the lyric, "He was born in the summer of his twenty-seventh year, coming home to a place he'd never been before." My mind, and my mother, thought I should be preparing for a serious career. My heart wanted to play music with my friends.

With my nights occupied by the music business, my days were free for my intellectual curiosities to resurface. One day I came upon a book about, of all people, Harry Houdini. In reading about his amazing escapes, I found myself wondering if he was simply a talented, inspired gymnast, or whether there was something truly magical going on. I began to wonder if there were forces active in the world that physics would not ultimately be able to explain. Harry Houdini was a trigger for me. Looking back, I see that 'Houdini hint' as serving to open me to possibilities that would later take a much more powerful form.

CHAPTER 4

PERSONAL INFLUENCERS

An oft quoted saying in some traditions is "When the student is ready, the teacher will appear." Though the origin of this quote seems to be obscure, I have seen it demonstrated over and over in my own life. In this chapter, I will discuss the appearance of non-traditional ideas in my search for knowledge about human possibilities. These ideas came to me through the four most important teachers who showed up in my experience, all through recommendations from friends.

Prem Rawat and meditation

Prem Rawat is the youngest son of an Indian guru and spiritual teacher from whom he inherited the title 'Satguru,' or 'True Master,' upon the father's passing. In 1973, when he was fourteen years old and living in the United States, I accepted an invitation to attend one of his gatherings. I felt in his presence the possibility that there might well be forces at work in my life that went far beyond anything I could then explain. In the same vein as the Beatles on their journeys with Maharishi Mahesh Yogi, though of course, without the fame and the cameras, I travelled to several places in the United States, as well as one trip abroad, to see and be with him, even if just for a moment. In his presence I felt a peace and joyfulness that I had never before experienced. Rawat said that those feelings were always within, and that with the practice of the meditation he taught I could feel them whenever I wanted.

I have practiced that meditation ever since, though (to quote John Denver once again), "Some days are diamonds, some days are stones." Yet the feeling of being called forth has persisted, the calling to continue searching for a deeper understanding of what it is to be a human being.

Influences from Carlos Castaneda

Carlos Castaneda published his first book, *The Teachings of Don Juan,* in 1968, and by his passing in 1998 he had brought forth eleven more. The books are narrated in the first person, and they relate experiences that took place in Mexico under the tutelage of a Yaqui Indian shaman who called himself Juan Matus.

Beginning in the early '70s and for decades thereafter, these books have been my favorite source of images and inspiration on this path of discovery. Castaneda reports that under the shaman's influence, and that of various natural psychoactive substances such as peyote and Datura, he experienced altered states of consciousness in which the world became fluid and lost the externality that forms the seemingly reliable context in which we live.

In Castaneda's telling, Matus performed numerous feats of sorcery, including changing into a crow, causing Castaneda's vehicle to vanish and reappear somewhere else, and transporting both himself and Castaneda a considerable distance in the blink of an eye. From a typical western perspective, we might well chalk all this up to an observer being in a hypnotic trance. When I first read these stories, I still believed steadfastly in the externality of the physical world. However, I found myself fascinated and somehow entranced by the possibility that the world I experience might not be quite as it seems to be.

Ultimately, after several years, I came to accept that Juan Matus actually acted and spoke as Castaneda reports he did. It's also possible, of course, that Castaneda made the whole thing up, as various debunkers have claimed. It really doesn't matter to me, because what I feel when I open myself to his accounts of the 'sorcerers' explanation'—for why and how things are the way they are—inspires me and continues to draw me forward.

Werner Erhard and the est Training

Werner Erhard was born John Paul Rosenberg in 1935. He took his new name from the Physicist, Werner Heisenberg and the German Economics Minister, Ludwig Erhard. He studied with the western interpreter of Zen Buddhism, Alan Watts, and in Japan with various Zen practitioners. After his involvement with a wide range of aspects of the so-called human potential movement, he founded his own experiential and transformational course, *est* (Latin for 'it is').

In 1976, I was introduced to the est Training, a four-day experience he originated in 1971. That course was designed to allow people to experience, in one culminating moment, the distinction between one's mind and oneself, and to make available the possibilities inherent in making that distinction. I experienced that moment of illumination as a profound transformation that will stay with me forever.

In Erhard's words (to the best of my recollection), the mind is "a linear array of multi-sensory total records of successive moments of now." He described the process by which one's experience, which happens in the moment, is immediately turned into a memory, complete with all the information that was delivered by our five senses as well as whatever we were feeling in that instant, the meaning we ascribed to the experience, and so on.

Erhard also described the human mind as a spinner of explanatory tales, decisions, and strategies about how to cope with the inevitable struggles of becoming assimilated into one's native culture as a child. According to the material presented in his work, we map these stories and decisions from childhood onto the challenges of adulthood without, in most cases, ever considering whether they are valid in the context of our adult experience, or indeed whether they were ever valid.

Functionally, the mind's job is to make records of everything that happens to us, to record the circumstances surrounding events that have significant positive and negative connotations, to make decisions about what circumstances to seek and to avoid, and to do all this to ensure our survival and our well-being. It's part of the standard equipment for human beings.

These records of our experiences are interlinked, in that the mind is constantly reminded of topics that are like the one being thought about, resulting in the so-called train of thought. Experientially, this is very much like the so-called rabbit hole into which one descends while clicking on links in our web browsers.

As a young person grows and becomes acculturated, the survival strategies created by the mind morph into strategies for the survival of the mind itself. The mind's primary method for insuring its own survival is to be right about the answers it gives us as we search for what to do next. As Juan Matus put it, "the guardian turns into a guard."

In the guise of a persona, with which we were arguably not born, we adults act in the world without ever considering that our personalities were to a large degree developed for a purpose. In examining my own childhood memories, I have come to see this purpose as one of coping with powerlessness. Powerlessness, after all, is the inevitable feeling of an infant which cannot take care of itself and which relies on bigger people for its every need. The result of this process is that our awareness of who we *really* are gets lost quite early in childhood. According to Erhard, by the age of seven, "it's all over." He went on to say that a human being will sacrifice anything and everything, including happiness, love, health, and self-expression, to obey the persistent priorities of the personality, and to steadfastly consider them to be the 'right' ones.

Erhard also presented 'field classes' where we could gain experiential knowledge of his precepts. In my first and only experience of the zip-line, which I initially dreaded, my mind screamed, "No way!" My body tensed uncomfortably, but my trust in the people managing the course was such that I stepped off the edge of a cliff, and my fear was immediately replaced by joy. This proved to be a visceral example of how learned fear responses to some situations can be released into a broader feeling of being taken care of.

That moment of transmuting fear into joy will also stay with me forever. It allowed me to realize for myself that I hear two voices: the loud one which constantly reminds me of what I can and can't do (and have), and the much softer one that encourages me to go beyond what I always thought were the limits of my personal possibilities.

Esther Hicks and Abraham

Over the years I have come across several people who describe themselves as channelers of non-physical entities. My first such encounter was with the writings of Jane Roberts, who channels a being identifying as Seth. Later, I heard Suzanne Giesemann speaking as Sanaya, and Lee Harris who brings forth 'the Zs.'

Esther Hicks, with her late husband Jerry Hicks, came upon and then thoroughly explored the possibility of channeling higher states of awareness through Esther's mind and voice. In seminars she conducts, she enters a unique kind of lucid meditative trance and speaks in a deeper, clearer, and more authoritative voice than that of her more 'normal' persona. She calls this voice 'Abraham.' In that voice, she speaks about how we humans are not simply these flesh and blood bodies but rather extensions of what she calls 'the energy that creates worlds.'

In 2010, I was introduced to her recordings of these sessions which are usually conducted before hundreds of people. I have listened to many of these seminars, and I attended one two-day experience. In terms of her explanation, human beings are extensions of loving, omniscient, non-physical energy, each of us having chosen many times to grow bodies in order to participate in this physical reality. The purpose of these physical incarnations is the experience of all that is possible in human existence, all of which this non-physical energy awareness treats as valuable, life-affirming, and devoid of judgement.

Central to Hicks's message is the Law of Attraction, the idea that thoughts, whether positive or negative, bring corresponding experiences into a person's life. 'Ask and It Is Given' can be thought of as a corollary to this law. I have been asking for deeper understanding of life as long as I can remember. This book is a result of that asking.

In this chapter I have described various ideas and methods employed by some of the teachers whom I have encountered in my search for understanding. I think one of the challenges of being a seeker of deeper wisdom is that spiritual teachers often use terminology that doesn't map clearly onto the vocabulary used by scientists ... or by regular folks, either. I have sometimes found that this leads to confusion and incomplete understanding. In addition, I have found that no single teacher has left me with what I consider to be the completely satisfying explanation I have always hoped to find. However, I have somehow synthesized all these ideas with some insights of my own and come to a framework that seems to hold up pretty well.

In the next chapter, I will return to my earlier proposition: when relying solely on information accessible to our five senses, we can never know about the essence of something we observe but only about how it behaves when we interact with it. That will lead to a discussion of the basics of first-semester high school physics, the understanding of the physical world that stood at the end of the 19th century. This basic level of physics matches up quite well with our shared, common-sense understanding of the world around us. I think this discussion will prove useful in grasping why 20th century physics represents such a radical transformation in our understanding of the world, and why we might want to acquire a new understanding of who *we* are in the light of this new way of looking at the world.

When the student is ready the teacher will appear. When the student is truly ready... The teacher will Disappear.

Lao Tzu

CHAPTER 5

CAN WE RE-IMAGINE THE PHYSICAL WORLD?

The world as a machine

In western culture, the traditional understanding of what we call 'reality' is that the physical world is what is real. All of us 'westerners' have been conditioned to that understanding, and it's pretty much universally accepted. It is also pretty much invisible to us, in the sense that we never think about it and never question whether it is actually true. It's an element of the 'water' we swim in.

All of us have been conditioned to think of the world, and the larger universe, as a machine. Machines tend to run according to their design, as formalized in the laws of physics, and they do so regardless of whether anybody is watching.

However, try looking at it this way: what we think of as the physical world is actually an interpretation of the information sent to our brain by our senses. Light that enters our eyes is converted to electrical impulses by rods and cones. These impulses are transmitted to our brains by the optic nerve. And our brains then make pictures out of these impulses, much like televisions create pictures out of the signals in the cable. These pictures, and sounds and so on, constitute an interpretation of sensory input. They become our *view* of the world.

We *assume* that this view is a more-or-less accurate picture of what's actually 'out there.' Then, we rely on these pictures of the physical world we have in our minds for all the strategies we use for getting along in life. The problem is, our interpretation of physical sensory data is conditioned by our experience of the past, by our habits of thought, by our beliefs, and by what we were told when we were young. All we have is our interpretation of what we see, and we all mistake that interpretation for what is actually there.

Well, what *is* actually there? The answer to that question is not nearly as straightforward as we might like it to be. Let's start with what seems to be a simpler question: how are objects made?

Interpreting the information from our five senses

I'm typing these words on a laptop that is resting on a kitchen counter. What is the essential nature of that surface? *What is it really?* Most people would say that it consists of some physical material, granite in this case. And what is the granite made of? The answer would be molecules or crystals of one or more substances, which are made of atoms, which are made of protons, neutrons, and electrons. That's just material from first semester high school physics.

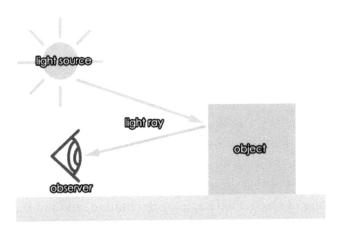

Now, what do I really see and feel when I look at or touch the kitchen counter? I see light bouncing off the counter and entering my eyes. I feel the effect of electrostatic forces in my fingertips. The scope of the information with which I can make sense of this material world is limited to what comes to me through my physical senses.

So, my interaction with the surface on which my laptop sits is limited to information about specific phenomena delivered to my brain by my senses. But what is it that makes those sensations into a kitchen counter? It is an *interpretation* of those sensations that 'makes' it into a counter. Without that interpretation, we would presumably still see and feel those sensations, but the counter would just appear to me as volume of marbled, brownish stuff that hurts if I bang into it and that seems to keep other stuff from falling on the floor. There is a layer of interpretation that lies between me and the object I am observing, and when I want to use that object (for example, to hold up my laptop), it is the interpretation with which I am interacting.

In this context, I am reminded of a story of the young child whose father is a television personality. The child sees his father on the television screen, and that image on the screen prompts the child to go around to the back of the set to find Daddy! Essentially, the TV is interpreting, or decoding, an electrical signal carried by a cable and rendering the resulting image on the screen. The signal being decoded consists of a vibration of what is called the electromagnetic field. The child, of course, does not yet realize that the image on the screen is merely a rendering of electrical data, a representation, and not the 'real' thing. I suggest that we do the same thing with the electrical input to our senses. My brain creates a picture of the world by interpreting the sensory data delivered to it, and I take that picture, or description, as if it were an external reality independent of my description.

Language and interpretation

According to Carlos Castaneda, Juan Matus said that we never experience the world itself. He said that instead, when we think or talk about our experience, it is the description of the world of which we think and speak.

> Think of this. The world doesn't yield to us directly; the description of the world stands in between. So, properly speaking, we are always one step removed, and our experience of the world is always a recollection of the experience. We are perennially recollecting the instant that has just happened, just passed. We recollect, recollect, recollect.

That is a vastly different idea of 'reality' than we're accustomed to, wouldn't you say? If we were to accept that idea as a premise, then the entire physical world we seem to be experiencing, that which we see, feel, taste, smell, and hear, would actually be a *description* consistent with our interpretation of the sensory data we receive. It would be a description held in memory, as opposed to a real world that exists independently of ourselves. And we can interact with one another because we share, to a sufficient degree, that interpretation.

In fact, it could be said that our language evolved for the express purpose of allowing us to participate in that interaction with others. That would explain why it is so hard to talk about whatever it is that might lie beyond or behind the description of the world: our language evolved to represent the description, and not the world itself.

We humans continually mistake our description of the world for the world itself. How might we have acquired that misinterpretation? Both Juan Matus and Werner Erhard essentially said that the description of the world was constantly reinforced by our parents, relatives, friends, and so on, from the moment we were born. That reinforcement takes the form of teaching a child his or her native language. In this view, the newborn starts out with a complex mix of sights and sounds and other sensations without the interpretive mechanism. He or she must then learn to perceive the world as *we* perceive it so as to be able to function in the world and interact with the rest of us. That process is called 'acculturation.'

WE WERE TAUGHT WORDS TO DESCRIBE THE EXPERIENCE OF OUR SENSES

In other words, *the child must become a member of the culture into which he or she is born.* That process of acquiring membership is carried out by absorbing and learning to perceive the descriptions offered. It occurs to me in this context that perhaps there are people among us in whom that membership status is not fully realized, whereupon we give them a diagnosis and attempt to treat them using various medical technologies. People on the autism spectrum come to mind here.

Physics and common sense

As you have read, I speak a bit about physics in this book. I do so in order to see if I can convince you, as I have been convinced, that what we call common sense, our shared 'knowledge' of the world we live in, is not a good indication of how the world actually works, let alone what it actually *is*. With the help of science, specifically quantum physics, I will make the case that common sense, or conventional wisdom, actually gives us a picture of the world that is, in a strict sense, wildly inaccurate.

In case you think that's a radical statement to make, consider that, in the arc of human history, it wasn't so long ago that people thought the world was flat. In fact, *everybody knew that*. And, if you were a seafaring man on the western coast of Europe prior to the 15th century, your travel options were rather limited as a result. You couldn't yet, for example, go to Queen Isabella in Castile and ask her for the funds to equip three ships for a westward voyage to the New World. She would have said, "Are you nuts? You'll fall off the edge!" Or something to that effect.

There are many examples from our history as a species when what everyone *knew* to be true turned out to be just plain wrong. And we have often clung tenaciously to our old views and resisted mightily any new understanding. Imagine asking Giordano Bruno, or Galileo, about their experiences when espousing the idea that the earth is not the center of the physical universe. Bruno got burned at the stake for his so-called transgression of church doctrine, and Galileo got confined to house arrest for his.

Ok, but wait. Those guys were primitive compared to us, right? They didn't have the benefit of all the calculations and experimental results, the physics, that have been done since their time. We are not under any of those powerful illusions like flat earth and geo-centrism, are we? Yet, what if we really *are* like those fish I spoke about earlier? What if we are all immersed in something invisible—more accurately, transparent—that not only colors everything we see but actually determines what we are *able* to see?

CHAPTER 6

CAN WE RE-IMAGINE THE HUMAN BEING?

Human beings as objects

In the previous chapter, we took a look at our commonly accepted idea of the physical world and at how we perceive that world. In that context, perception is understood as the awareness and exploration of what is out there in a world that exists independently of us human beings.

In this book, I'm suggesting that what we think of as the real world, the physical world, is instead an interpretation of sensory input, a *description*, which is conditioned by our past experience and our belief systems. This represents a fundamental shift in how human beings are related to the world. It also compels a re-imagining of what a human being really is. And just as in the last chapter, we'll start with what we all already 'know' about that subject.

Classically speaking, according to my dictionary, a human being is a member of the species *Homo sapiens*, distinguished from other animals by "superior mental development, power of articulate speech, and upright stance." This distinction, especially the part about upright stance, implies that a human being is essentially a human body which is differentiated from other animal bodies by those characteristic attributes.

You can pull up a diagram that shows a classification scheme for animals found on Earth.

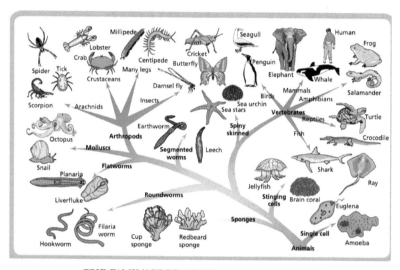

THE FAMILY TREE OF THE ANIMAL KINGDOM

Let's look a bit more closely at such a scheme. It is a classification method by which you can try to understand the 'origin of species,' in Darwin's phrase.

When you classify creatures in the standard fashion, you deal with things like kingdom, phylum, class, order, family, genus, and species. It's a complicated system that looks like a tree with a trunk, thick branches, thinner branches, and so on. And at the end of one of those branches, there we are. Right?

You could say this definition of human being is object-oriented. We think of ourselves as objects standing out against the background of the world. One of the problems with this object-oriented view of human beings is that it locks us into separation and competition with one another. And not the kind of competition that makes each of us better, but the kind that creates winners and losers, haves and have-nots, us and them. Well, how else could we look at what a human being actually *is*? When we use the word 'self,' what are we referring to?

What is a 'self'?

The dictionary defines the adjective 'sentient' as "having the power of perception by the senses; conscious." It seems pretty clear that the word 'sentient' applies to us. But what is it that *has* that power of perception? Is it the body, or is it something more fundamental and more abstract?

As I noted earlier, I've investigated a number of metaphysical disciplines in my search for a deeper understanding of human consciousness. Each of those disciplines offers an answer to the question, '*What is it* that is aware or conscious of all the sensory input and resulting interpretation?' The answers almost always include the word 'self.' However, many who are versed in this subject matter have spoken of the difficulty of talking about that self directly. In fact, it appears that our entire linguistic arsenal exists to describe what the self observes or has experienced, and not the self itself!

Let me see if I can make this difficulty a bit clearer. First, I think it will be useful here to introduce a term that points to a powerful abstraction. The dictionary defines the word 'domain' in a number of ways; the one I'll use here is, "a realm or range of personal knowledge."

Werner Erhard said that we humans operate in three fundamentally different domains: Having, Doing, and Being. All of us are familiar with the first two, and arguably very few of us have much familiarity with the last one. 'Having' encompasses not only physical objects but also memories, thoughts, and emotions. Similarly, 'Doing' involves not only physical actions but also observing, thinking, and remembering.

I have come to understand that human language was developed for working with the domains of Having and Doing, and not for the domain of Being. In this chapter, we will bear in mind the difficulty of speaking of one domain, in this case Being or the self, with language developed for other domains. What I can do, however, is approach the nature of the self by drawing some distinctions about what the self is not. I have encountered several of these distinctions in my inquiry, and I'll present some of those in the following paragraphs.

During his est Training, Werner Erhard referred to the distinction experienced in that special moment when the self is distinguished from the mind. When I arrived at that point in the course, my mind instantly went on the defensive, calling the entire proceedings 'evil.' In that experience of revelation, as I now recall it, I saw my mind as something other than who I am. From that perspective, I watched my mind thrashing about for a way to explain, and actually to hide, what just happened. In that moment, it was clear to me that the self and the mind are actually distinct from one another. In the years since that moment, I have realized with ever-increasing clarity that the voice I've always heard in my head, my 'thinking' voice, isn't actually me. It just sounds like me! Erhard referred to that voice as 'It.'

Eckhart Tolle, in his book, *The Power of Now*, tells the story of the moment he suddenly acquired a deeper understanding of a thought that had kept repeating itself in his mind. The thought was, "I cannot live with myself any longer." He continued, "Then suddenly I became aware of what a peculiar thought it was. 'Am I one or two? If I cannot live with myself, there must be two of me: the I and the self that I cannot live with.'" This theme, that there are two of us, runs through all the examples in this chapter.

Juan Matus told Carlos Castaneda that there are two parts to who we are. He said the 'sorcerers' explanation' calls those two parts the Tonal and the Nagual. The Tonal, he said, consists of everything we can name or even conceive of. That part of ourselves is responsible for holding the description of the world in place so that there is continuity and coherence to the world we perceive and act in. Our language is designed to speak exclusively about the Tonal and its doings, what he called 'the human inventory.'

Matus went on to say that the Nagual, on the other hand, is responsible for creation. It cannot effectively be spoken about or described. It can only be witnessed, and only in the moment in which it is witnessed, before the Tonal has turned the Nagual's appearance into another element of its inventory, another memory. According to Matus, one way to describe what it is to be a 'sorcerer' is that one knows how to get to the Nagual. Once there, the Nagual expresses itself according to the mood of the sorcerer, and its effects cannot be predicted. If the sorcerer is joyful, for example, its effects will bring great joy.

Here, Matus has described our Having two parts of ourselves and the Doing of each of them. He does not refer explicitly to the Being which has these two parts, other than to say that the two parts to who we are, the Tonal and the Nagual, comprise (as he put it rather dramatically) the "totality of the Being that is going to die."

Esther Hicks, when channeling Abraham, also speaks of two parts of who we are. In terms of this description, there

is first our 'Inner Being, who we really are,' and then there is
the part of us that's focused on this time-space reality, on our
human Being-ness. Yet, there is no description of that Inner
Being that we really are. There is a description of the thoughts
It thinks, and how they can be distinguished from the thoughts
we entertain in our human minds. Once again, we see reference
to the Doing of these parts of ourselves, but not to their Being.

In summary, so far

It is clear to me that the world we think is 'out there,' the one we
experience, is actually an interpretation we make of the complex
mix of perceptual input to which we're tuned. We believe that
we *are* our bodies, but I'm convinced that our bodies are part of
the world that is a product of our observation. That realization
leads to the conclusion that *we* are not objects among the larger
world of objects, as our bodies are. We are more accurately the
container in which those objects, including our bodies, show up.[1]

---

[1] I have already referred to the difficulty of speaking about one domain
with language developed for another. The word 'container' here is a
perfect example. It belongs naturally in the domain of Having, as in
something which has contents. In terms of that usage, the current
paradigm has it that our bodies contain our awareness, thoughts, and
feelings. Therefore, we believe that those human qualities must reside
in our brains and nervous systems. Here, however, in the context of
this new explanation, the presence of our bodies in our awareness is
a function of interpretation and they therefore properly reside 'in'
our awareness. I thus borrow the word 'container' and adapt it for
my purpose.

CHAPTER 7

THE WORLD AS A CONTINUOUS FLOW OF INTERPRETATION

Our interpretation of sensory input occurs as a continuous flow. The voice I distinguished in the est Training, 'It,' continuously describes what I have just experienced. Until I was 29 years old, I thought it was my voice, and I believed that its interpretation was the world itself. But during that year, something happened that changed my view of the world, and of myself, forever. I would like to present that story here.

An Extra-Ordinary Experience

One day in 1974, I bought an International Scout in Southern California and began to drive it back home to Colorado. I had several criteria for what car to buy. It had to have room for a bunch of music equipment, and it had to have four-wheel drive. It was ok with me that it was the color of the desert and wasn't very attractive. What I didn't consider at all was fuel economy.

Back then, I was based in Aspen, making a living as a musician. When I say, 'making a living,' I mean paying rent and buying food, and occasionally having some extra spending

MY '73 INTERNATIONAL SCOUT

money. I didn't have a credit card, and I didn't have a cell phone. And on that particular day, I had what I thought was enough cash to make the trip home.

As I drove to the San Francisco Bay area to visit friends, I started thinking about the rather poor gas mileage, the price of gas, the miles to go, and how much money I had in my wallet. I knew it would be a closer call than I had anticipated. But I had to get home!

As I prepared to depart Berkeley for Aspen, I stopped at a filling station to top off the tank. Those were the days when you could look in the pipe and see the surface of the liquid, and I could see it shimmering in the sunlight.

Though I set off on my journey with a light heart, I gradually felt that lightness disappear. I was having a persistent conversation with myself, worrying about how much gas this car used and about whether I would actually have enough money to get home. This frightened me. I had never experienced being alone on the road and having to hitchhike or whatever else might be required if I ran out of gas. I felt fear in my stomach and in my chest, and as I drove, it became more and more oppressive.

Religion of any kind was not part of my childhood experience, and I had never before thought of praying to whomever or whatever might be listening. But on that morning, I did just that, essentially confessing my 'sins,' such as the arrogance of my refusal to quit the music business and get a 'real' job, my insistence that I was right and my mother was wrong regarding my attitude about money, and about the way I was living my life in general.

In the next moment I clearly heard a strong, powerful Voice that spoke with complete authority. It said,

"Don't worry Larry, we'll get you home."

Immediately there was no conversation in my head. I knew that something very profound had happened, and in some sense the way I viewed the world had fundamentally shifted, though at the time I had no words to express that shift. My heart was beating a little faster, and I felt a lightness and something I might have called breathless anticipation.

Realizing that I was now fully present in that car, in the Central Valley of California, noticing the scenery, hearing the car's noises, and aware of my breathing, I felt a calmness come over me I had rarely experienced. The usual mental chatter, which I sometimes call the internal dialog, 'It,' was conspicuous by its absence. I experienced that silence with feelings of great relief. Somehow, I knew I was ok, and that this situation would work itself out one way or another.

As you might expect, the silence didn't last, and I was soon indulging in my usual mental chatter. At some point, I happened to glance at my gas gauge. I saw that it had not moved from its 'full' reading, and by my calculations the car by now should have used about a quarter-tank. My first reaction was something like, "Oh great, now the gas gauge isn't working. I'll have to get that fixed… although, since I know how many miles-per-gallon I'm getting, I can still figure out when I need gas."

Shortly thereafter, the gas gauge began to fall. Now my thinking was, "Well ok, it doesn't register the first quarter-tank drop, so I can compensate for whatever it reads. No problem."

As I approached the foothills of the Sierra Nevada, I decided to stop and top off the tank again. The gauge now read three-quarters full, and my mental calculations told me it really was half full. I pumped the gas, and as I stood there, I was still feeling some of the relief I had felt when the mental chatter had stopped. The pump clicked off, and as I hung up the hose, I looked at the reading. The car had taken a quarter-tank of gas, not the half-tank I was expecting.

I looked in the gas pipe, and there was the surface of the liquid shimmering as before.

A strange mixture of disbelief and complete trust washed over me. On the one hand, I had no way to explain what had just happened, and on the other, I was again feeling that everything was fine. In terms of what I see now, the world had stopped for me. By that I mean, the normal flow of events, and most importantly the flow of interpretation of those events, stopped for me, because my rational mind had no answer, no explanation. I had the clear thought that I had just experienced something outside the boundaries I had always assumed were dictated by 'reality,' by the laws of physics.

The power of our idea of the world

The books that Carlos Castaneda wrote about Juan Matus tell the story of Castaneda's interactions with a man who called himself a sorcerer. These days we might call him a shaman. There are 'tales of power' in those books that relate incidents that a first-time reader might have a hard time accepting as real. For me, they're worth reading about even if they aren't real because of Castaneda's skill as a writer. I wouldn't call those works self-help books. For me, however, the value of his books is that while reading them I feel the 'whispering' of that deeper self that I actually am. For that feeling alone, I am grateful to him.

However, there is another idea that I take from those stories that is relevant to our fundamental question about what it is to be a human being. And it emerges from the realization that our *idea* of the world is what allows us to experience the world as we do. On that day in 1974, when I had no choice but to conclude that my car had just travelled a considerable distance without using any gas, something about the world stopped. Visually, of course, it was all there. I could see the car and the level of the liquid in the pipe. I could hear sounds around me. I could feel the pump handle in my hand. Yet, in Matus's terms, my understanding of the way the world works had shifted. I can see now that what we call the world is a continuous, uninterrupted flow of interpretation. And in that moment, all those years ago, that flow simply stopped. Juan Matus called an experience such as that one, 'stopping the world.'

Castaneda relates numerous experiences of similar disruptions of the normal flow of events. As he tells it, his first such experience, taking place in the Mexican desert, involved having a two-way conversation with a coyote. The next day, Matus told Castaneda,

> What stopped inside you yesterday was what people have been telling you the world is like. You see, people tell us from the time we are born that the world is such and such and so and so, and naturally we have no choice but to see the world the way people have been telling us it is ... Yesterday the world became as sorcerers tell you it is. In order to [know who we really are], one must learn to look at the world in some other fashion [than the way we've been taught], and the only other fashion I know is the way of a sorcerer.

I don't spend time in the Mexican desert, and to my knowledge I have never met a sorcerer. But I have discovered that everyday life gives me opportunities to see the world in terms different from those of the description I was taught. I have never had a sorcerer around to guide me, so I've had to learn to do this by myself. As a result, it has been a long, slow process and required a great deal of patience and persistence.

CHAPTER 8

A CLOSER LOOK AT THE PHYSICAL WORLD

Previously, I have related a handful of details about my study of physics, a journey that gave me an understanding of how scientists talk about the physical world. When I left that formal study, I thought it had been somewhat wasted: preparation for a career path that ultimately didn't suit me. It now appears to have been perfect preparation for the work that has led me to this book.

During the 20th century, people who study the physical world in great and painstaking detail were forced to modify, or abandon entirely, assumptions that had been considered true for centuries, assumptions that were derived from, and were therefore consistent with, 'common sense.' Many of the conclusions they adopted in their efforts to understand what they were observing are confusing, contradictory, and downright mystifying. In this chapter, I will describe some of these experiment-driven shifts in our collective thinking about the world.

As you may have gathered, I really enjoy reading, thinking, and talking about physics. My purpose in including it in this book is twofold: first, it's to try to persuade you that our belief in the ultimate reality of the world, what might be called the 'seniority' of the world with respect to us humans, is just not sustained by modern physics. And as a related purpose, it is to further expand upon the idea that using 'common-sense' experience as a guide to our understanding how the world, and life, actually work is really misleading.

Physics early in the 20th century

As the 20th century began, an inventory of the ideas which physicists used to make sense of the physical world would have included the following. First, there was matter, the stuff you can see, taste, and so on, with your five senses. Matter, "any object, fluid, or gas under consideration" (according to the dictionary), came to be thought of as a collection of small chunks called atoms, which themselves consisted of even smaller chunks called protons, neutrons, and electrons.

These smaller chunks would later be said to be composed of still smaller chunks. In any case, it was believed that with clever enough experimentation, we could eventually come upon chunks that were fundamental, indivisible building blocks from which the material world is constructed. It was also thought that if you could determine the location as well as the speed and direction of motion of each of these indivisible particles, you could with enough time and effort (and computing power) determine the organization of the universe at each moment in either the past or the future.

Second in our physicist's inventory were forces. In the frame of reference of which we are speaking, forces can act upon matter at a distance. For example, gravity was seen to act upon objects not physically adjacent to each other and with no visible connection, such as the earth and the sun. By observing the motion of these objects, Sir Isaac Newton, in the 17th century, arrived at a description of gravity that would allow us to predict with great accuracy their future motions and positions. However, among Newton and his contemporaries, the nature of these forces themselves and their origins or causes continued to elude understanding.

And finally, these particles and forces were seen to exist in space and time. Space was thought to be nothing but an abstract idea, a way of referring to the emptiness that seems to be filled, though sparsely on a large scale, with matter and forces. Perhaps its function was just a way to organize matter. Similarly, time was thought to be just an idea whose function was to organize events chronologically.

The inventory I've just outlined constitutes a paradigm. According to the dictionary, a paradigm is "a framework containing the basic assumptions, ways of thinking, and methodology that are commonly accepted by members of a scientific community." This paradigm had an interesting feature which went largely unnoticed: it was a *story*, one whose truth was not only commonly accepted but also taken for granted. It was assumed that this framework represented *the way things actually are*. As I told you earlier, when I was studying this stuff in school, I suspected that we might not be able to know the way things actually are, but only the way they show up in the picture we assemble out of sensory input. I know, that's a very subtle distinction. However, it turns out to be a crucial distinction, as I hope you will see.

Anyway, during the early part of the 20th century, this paradigm was put to the test and was found to be inadequate. You could even say it fell on its face.

The breakdown of classical physics

Early in the last century, careful experiments revealed that light doesn't behave as common sense would have you expect. Specifically, measuring the speed of light always gives the same answer no matter how fast you move relative to its source. Let me see if I can show you how confusing that result can be to common sense.

In the case of all phenomena on a human scale, interactions with moving objects are far less challenging if you match their speed with your own. Consider as an example the International Space Station. It is moving relative to the launchpad at Cape Canaveral at a bit more than 17,000 miles per hour. And yet, we can send humans there with a rocket that safely approaches the station at about one inch per second. That's because the relative speed of the station and the rocket changes between the rocket's launch and the rendezvous. But in the case of a ray of light, that change doesn't happen. No matter how fast you travel, you can never even begin to catch up to that light ray.

Albert Einstein was the first to realize that our ideas of space and time had to change to account for the inescapable experimental result that the speed of light is always measured to be the same. His theory of special relativity resulted in space and time no longer being thought of as abstract containers. Instead, they needed to be thought of as entities with dynamics of their own, expanding and contracting according to the state of motion of anyone observing them. If you think about this situation, you may see that it's not at all intuitive!

Continuing our glance at the physicist's inventory of the past century, we come to forces. The idea that forces act across distance with no visible means of connection gave way to a new conception, that of the field. A field, in physics, permeates all of space and in so doing connects objects at a distance. An example would be the electromagnetic field, which connects charged objects and carries their attraction and repulsion. Another would be the gravitational field, which connects massive objects and carries their mutual attraction. Einstein re-imagined gravity as the warping of space and time (which he combined into 'spacetime') by the presence of matter. Because of his work, physicists now think of matter as telling spacetime how to warp and spacetime telling matter how to move.

Walter Isaacson, in his extensively researched and wonderfully written biography of Albert Einstein, wrote of this revolution in thought as follows: "With his special theory of relativity, Einstein had shown that space and time did not have independent existences, but instead formed a fabric of spacetime. Now, with his general version of the theory, this fabric of spacetime became not merely a container for objects and events. Instead, it had its own dynamics that were determined by, and in turn helped to determine, the motion of objects within it."[2]

THE WARPING OF SPACE BY HEAVY BODIES

---

[2] Walter Isaacson, *Einstein: His Life and Universe* (New York: Simon & Schuster Paperbacks, 2007), 223.

The fields with which we are most familiar, the gravitational and electromagnetic fields, are dynamic entities. They not only contain objects and their interactions, but also sustain wave behavior, much as we see in water. Waves in the electromagnetic field are called light. And gravitational waves have recently been detected for the first time, giving us a new way to study celestial collisions on the scale of stars and galaxies. Those gigantic collisions really do make waves!

As experiments became increasingly sophisticated, scientists could also examine matter on smaller and smaller scales. The previously held idea that there are a definite number of fundamental particles, whose position and velocity could be accurately determined, began to break down. It was ultimately found, for example, that at these small scales, you can't accurately determine a particle's position and velocity at the same time. This is called the Heisenberg Uncertainty Principle. It was also found that particles can and do pop into and out of existence. That's called 'quantum fluctuations.' Particles can and do behave like waves or particles, depending on the experiment performed. This is referred to as 'wave-particle duality.' Objects can affect each other instantaneously over great distances, a phenomenon called 'quantum non-locality.' And so on.

Quantum theory gives you reliable, experimentally verifiable answers to any questions you might ask of it. It has proven its validity through applications in current technology. It has been said that if physicists hadn't been working on quantum mechanics in the '20s and '30s, we would never have gotten transistors in the '50s and '60s. And we wouldn't have cellphones and computers today.

However, quantum theory also says some very strange things, some very non-intuitive things, about the world!

Here are three quotes from *Quantum Enigma,* a book by two lecturers at the University of California, Bruce Rosenblum and Fred Kuttner, published by Oxford University Press, 2011.

- "Quantum theory tells us that an object can be in two [or more] places at the same time."
- "The object's existence at the particular place where it happens to be found becomes an actuality only upon its observation."
- "Quantum theory thus denies the existence of a physically real world independent of its observation."

In other words, quantum theory flatly contradicts the idea that we are observers of a world that doesn't care whether or not we observe it. It suggests instead that observers, you and I, cannot be separated from that which is under observation.

So, once more, what *is* actually 'there'? And, more generally, what is actually *real?*

Quantum physics and possibilities

It turns out that, according to quantum theory, what is actually 'there' is a limitless field of possibilities, otherwise known as the quantum field. The theory makes this idea more formal. It is formulated to refer not to how things actually behave, but rather to what the results of observations of those things *are likely to be.*

That's another very subtle distinction. Let me repeat it: quantum theory is formulated to refer not to how things *actually behave,* but rather to what the results of *observations of their behavior are likely to be.* You would think that any successful theory of the universe would explain what's actually there. But here we have a theory that only explains what you're likely to see!

Let's explore this idea for a few moments. Prior to the discovery of the quantum laws, classical physics did describe almost perfectly how things behave, at least within the range of direct human experience. However, as I said before, classical laws describe the behavior of inanimate objects, forces, and fields, and they do so without reference to anybody actually observing that behavior. Thus, these laws have nothing to say about the consciousness (us) that's actually doing the observing.

Quantum laws, however, are all about the results of observations. Quantum laws predict the results of observations of physical systems, and as far as we know they do so with complete accuracy.

And right there, consciousness is inseparable from the field of physics. Isn't it rather meaningless to talk about the results of experiments or observations without implicitly referring to the conscious being that's doing the experimenting?

Now, it's true that classical ideas from physics and chemistry have been used to try to explain the origin of thoughts and feelings, as well as the consciousness that's aware of them. These explanations are formulated in terms of the nervous system and the brain. Most scientists seem to believe that experience, and in fact life itself, must ultimately be a product of things, such as atoms and molecules, that most people would say aren't in themselves alive. In other words, take physics and chemistry, add enough complexity and just the right combination of environmental factors, and if you're lucky, you get life, and eventually, human experience.

I have a hard time with the idea that you can get life, and then consciousness, from non-living raw materials. When we transitioned to quantum laws, however, it seems to me that this whole issue should have gone away. The science shows that observation is the basis for the appearance of the physical world. And yet most scientists still insist that the physical world must somehow create the consciousness that is required for the observations to exist.

Since we live in a world that's essentially created by observation, in studying the way the world behaves we are actually studying perception and, therefore, ourselves. When scientists confront the combination of the complexity as well as the beauty of the world, the emotional reaction on the part of many seems to be confusion and frustration that some of the world's 'secrets' appear to defy explanation. Yet I think the more appropriate reaction is awe. I think it is deserving of awe and deep reverence that we are capable of perceiving that beauty and complexity simply by interpreting the electrical signals that reach our brains.

People use the word 'miracle' to refer to situations where we sometimes emerge intact and even enhanced from seemingly impossible circumstances. But maybe the real miracle is that we not only perceive a beautiful world but that we perceive a world at all, and that we can actually agree on what we're observing. And furthermore, I think we have to ask, "How can the physical world be what is real *when it requires perception in order to come into being?*"

Human experience

Let's return to human experience. It's pretty difficult to define experience, especially in terms of the physical world. But you know it when you have it! I suggest that experience, and thoughts, and feelings, are what is real. When you awaken from a dream, the scene you were dreaming vanishes ... but the experience of the dream remains. Sometimes you can feel the feelings you had in the dream for the rest of the day.

After more than a hundred years of debate, quantum scientists still believe that the physical world is a law-based machine. They have yet to agree on how to get from a field of probabilities to what we actually experience, to what we think of as reality. Perhaps the time will come when these women and men of science finally discover for themselves that we cannot fully explain reality without talking about consciousness. Maybe then, more of them will begin to consider the implications of realizing that there is no world apart from its observation, that the world 'out there' isn't what it seems to be, and that we are so much more than we imagine *ourselves* to be.

If you take into consideration the arguments in this chapter, you may see that we are discussing a new and completely different paradigm with which we can look at the world. We have fields that sustain vibrations (light, gravity, electrical, magnetic, and so on) and we use our five senses to interpret and convert those vibrations into our picture of reality. And that *picture or description* of reality is not the same as whatever might actually be 'out there.' In fact, it's as different from what the universe might actually be as is the glossy picture of a stack of pancakes on the menu at the pancake house from that stack of pancakes that you're eating! And, I might add, it's about as satisfying relative to what human life could be.

CHAPTER 9

REALITY AS A STORY

So far in this book, when I have talked about reality, I have considered the concrete, physical sort of reality with which we are all familiar. Now I would like to propose the idea that there exists a different kind of reality, which I will call abstract reality, that lies behind the physical one. I'll explain later why I think this other reality is worth considering. For now, let's just focus on getting a feel for it.

Whenever I attempt to deal with stuff that's really abstract, I like to have a metaphor to work with; otherwise, it's just too hard to wrap my mind around it. So, I like to use the idea of the film projector, even though there is now a generation that has never seen one.

A metaphor from the movies

What are the elements of a film-based movie house? First, before we turn on the projector, we have a big white screen. That screen has no content; it's just a place to focus our attention when we get some content going. Next, we have a light bulb that projects pure white light onto the screen. White light consists of all the frequencies of visible light, from red at the low end

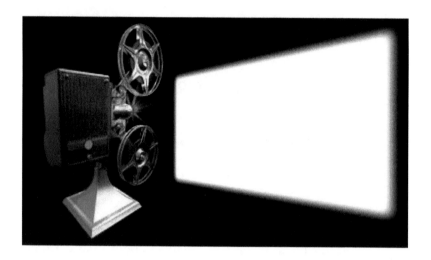

to blue at the high end, that added together make up what we perceive as white.

OK, so we have white light and a white screen. So far, it's a really boring movie! The last element is the film, which gets threaded into the projector. The film allows us to project the movie onto the screen. It does that by blocking, or filtering out, various frequencies of light at various points on the film and allowing all the other frequencies to pass through it. So, the visual portion of the movie is created by a process of removing some of the light. And what's left is what we see on the screen. Now, if we were to ask ourselves what is more real, the movie or the film strip, I think we can see that the film strip is more tangible, more real than the movie. If the power goes off, for example, the movie disappears but the film strip remains.

The elements of this metaphor are the light bulb, the film, and the screen. The light bulb, with its white light, represents all possibilities. The screen, or more accurately, what's projected onto the screen, represents the reality we perceive. And the film represents this 'abstract reality' I'm proposing that we discover. It is abstract from our human perspective because we can't see it with our eyes. We see with our eyes only the *results* of subtracting from all possibilities (of various colors and brightness) those upon which we are not now focusing. The purpose of this chapter is to focus on that metaphorical film strip. I will argue that if we want to understand how our reality is created, we have to talk about abstraction, the 'film' that lies behind what we all think of as reality.

Abstractions – filters of reality

First of all, what is abstraction? The dictionary defines an abstraction as "a generalized idea or theory developed *from* concrete examples of an event." It can be concluded from this definition that the concrete examples of events come first. Then, the idea or theory is abstracted from these experiences. In other words, it is an after-the-fact process, occurring after those realities are perceived by you and me. I'll call these kinds of ideas 'explanatory abstractions.'

Consider, for example, the notion of danger. Danger is an abstraction, rather than a concrete reality. Nobody has ever seen danger the same way we see tables and chairs. A child may be pushed in the school hallway or bitten by a neighborhood dog, or she may observe someone else having a similar experience. For the child, of course, these events constitute concrete realities. The child will likely then derive the abstraction of danger from actual experience, such as the push or the bite, and express it in the story she inevitably tells about that experience.

Alternatively, she may derive the idea of danger from anecdotal evidence, such as when parents, who themselves consider the world a dangerous place, repeatedly warn their children about the many bad things that could happen to them and the strategies they should use to protect themselves. In either case, the child absorbs those stories into her description of the world and, through repeatedly telling those stories, comes to feel that the world is to one degree or another a dangerous place.

Now let's consider another type of abstraction. This idea arises from a different interpretation of reality, wherein the world we experience, with its apparent concrete realities, is actually a description that we've mistaken for the world it describes. It's the picture of the pancakes on the menu, not the breakfast itself.

In life, all we really have to work with is a *description* of how the world behaves when we interact with it. We all came to rely on that description, because it afforded us a way to get what we want and avoid physical and emotional harm in the process. More generally, it allows us to make sense of, and bring order to, what would otherwise be a bewildering and virtually infinite array of sensations and impressions. The broad outline of our description of the world was inherited from our culture as we became its newest members. Because we inherited the basis of our description of the world as we were learning language, we never stopped to examine the assumptions it was built on. It became the water we swim in.

We depend on our description of the world for everything we perceive. As a result, nothing new can be allowed to threaten that description; we hold onto it with all our might. So, what happens when we encounter new events and new people, and we form new memories? Any new experiences are *forced* to fit into our preexisting explanatory or descriptive scheme, into what we already know to be true. *Even though this description is abstract, it nevertheless limits what we are able to experience, what we're able to accept as being real.*

In this view, abstraction (our description) actually precedes the appearance of those 'realities.' From this vantage point, *abstractions lead to concrete realities*, and not the other way around. Objects become objects through the process of interpretation of sensory input. I call these abstractions 'causal abstractions,' as opposed to the explanatory abstractions I described earlier.

That is a radical reinterpretation of reality: abstractions (our description of the world, our beliefs about it) cause and shape perception. Again, I propose it not as a fact but rather as a working hypothesis. If it turned out to be a useful hypothesis, how might it show up in our experience?

Possibility as a causal abstraction

The word 'possibility' points to a causal abstraction few of us have examined, and which I think it's worthwhile to think about in the context of the seer's explanation. Let's consider what the word 'possibility' means. Referring to the dictionary, we read that possibility means "the state or fact of being possible," or "something that is possible." The word 'possible,' in turn, means "that which can be, exist, happen, be done, or be used." In terms of what we all think, what is possible is conveyed as conventional wisdom, or 'what everybody knows.'

Here is a practical and timely example. Suppose you, like many other people, believe that on a day-to-day basis in today's economy, it's not possible to have a rich choice of job opportunities. Suppose further that you have looked for work in this type of economy, and that your experience looking for a job has shown you that, in fact, there aren't a lot of good choices. Your experience provides ample demonstration of the accuracy of your belief. This suggests that 'what everybody knows' is constantly reinforced by our individual experience, and as a result we constantly consider ourselves to be right about our expectations.

Consider 'what everybody knows' about the economy. Everybody 'knows' that there is one economy that we're essentially stuck with. Then, we talk about why some people do better in that economy than others. We tend to conclude that the degree of relative prosperity each of us experiences is due to some combination of education, skill sets, and raw accidents of birth … or just plain luck.

In other words, in terms of the reality we all believe in, 'the economy' is a *thing*. But what if the economy, like every other aspect of the world we are describing, is a story, a description based on our *interpretation* of what we see and hear about it? According to that hypothesis, the economy each of us experiences is the result of viewing economic activity through the lens or window provided by what we believe is possible, or the possibility which each of us has accepted as being *real*.

Let's flesh this out a bit further. In the context of the possibility that most of us have bought into, the one we inherited from our culture, very few of us experience both adequate income *and* the personal freedom to determine how to spend our time. Everybody 'knows' that you have to restrict the uses you make of your time and personal freedom to those that don't conflict with your job. In terms of my hypothesis that we mistake our description of reality for reality itself, that choice is the one we must make between options that we (and our culture) have accepted as being *real*.

However, how would you tell the difference between being *right* about your beliefs about the economy, on the one hand, and the economy simply reflecting your beliefs about it, on the other? Here's a different way of asking that question: virtually all of us subscribe to the idea that the economy is something external to us that we just have to deal with. Is that externality real, or is it just a belief most of us have?

The birth of possibility

Now consider a completely different understanding of possibility from the one we inherited from our culture. Werner Erhard made, I think, a particularly useful distinction between options and possibilities. He proposed that we consider options as the range of choices that are dictated or allowed by a particular possibility. Further, he suggested that from time to time, human beings invent new possibilities, truly new sets of options, in what he called 'an act of existential courage.'

Erhard said that a possibility that's counter to the prevailing worldview has to be declared by a human being as an individual act of creation. By way of illustration, he pointed out that not so long ago in our collective history, 'human rights' did not exist.

Kings had rights, priests had rights, but ordinary human beings did not have rights. Now, of course, 'human rights' is part of our daily lexicon.

I think that long ago there occurred a more fundamental shift in the story people tell about who they are. I am referring to the much earlier era when a multitude of oral traditions were set down in writing over a period of time in what we now refer to as the Old Testament of the Bible. Thomas Cahill, in his beautifully written book *The Gifts of the Jews—How a Tribe of Desert Nomads Changed the Way Everyone Thinks and Feels*, argues that the story set down in the Old Testament reflects a truly monumental shift in the stories we human beings tell about ourselves.

Cahill notes that before that Old Testament story came alive, human life was thought of as "a vision of the cosmos that was profoundly cyclical." Cahill quotes Henri-Charles Puech, speaking of ancient Greek thought in his book, *Man and Time:*

> No event is unique, nothing is enacted but once ... every event has been enacted, is enacted, and will be enacted perpetually; the same individuals have appeared, appear, and will appear at every turn of the circle.

In other words, prior to the Old Testament, the story that people (in particular, the Greeks) told of human life was one of perpetual repetition, in which each generation acted out parts that had already been performed countless times before. Metaphorically, you could visualize this story as two-dimensional, because a circle can be drawn on a flat piece of paper.

But the story of Abraham, Moses, and those who came after, includes a completely life-altering innovation: the *possibility* of better things to come. In short, the people who created this new story essentially invented possibility itself, and in particular the possibility of the future being an improvement over the past.

In reading Cahill, it seems to me that this may have been the most powerful new thought, the most powerful evolution of our story, that human beings have ever created. It brought the human story into three dimensions, as if the circle had just revealed itself to be a helix.

Again, my proposition is that what we deal with on a daily basis is a description of the world that we've mistaken for the world itself. In the light of this formulation, we could consider that the world we experience, a *description*, is made not just of abstractions as I suggested earlier, but of that particular class of abstractions called possibilities.

I should note that we are born into an established possibility, which Juan Matus called the 'Tonal of the times.' This possibility determines, or allows, all the options that people in our era consider real, even if a particular person doesn't consider one or more of those options available to themselves. This default possibility doesn't require an act of declaration to be present as physical manifestation. It just *is*, for everyone who accepts the reality typically described by those who teach us language. Unless the Tonal of the times shifts, additional possibilities must first be imagined and then declared by individual human beings, so as to be available to themselves and perhaps to others.

Declaring and creating new possibilities

Well, what does it mean to declare a new possibility? I believe that this is an important aspect of the effort to understand what it is to be a human being. Speaking a new possibility aloud, or writing it down, doesn't seem to be sufficient—think of New Years' resolutions, for example. Before we explore that question philosophically, let's look for some images that may help to clarify things.

Recall the example I offered earlier of the television that interprets an electrical signal and renders it on the screen and in the loudspeakers as your favorite program. How does the TV interpret a signal that the cable delivers to it? In broad, non-technical terms, the TV contains an electronic circuit that has a tunable resonant frequency. By subtly varying the values of certain components of that circuit, its resonant frequency can be tuned precisely to that of the chosen channel.

How might we visualize this idea of resonance? Perhaps you have had the experience of turning up the volume on your stereo and hearing something rattle on the other side of the

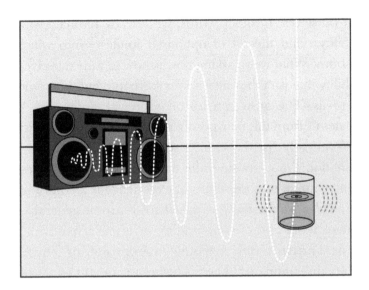

room. Or maybe the neighbors have turned up *their* stereo and all you hear is the bass guitar. These examples demonstrate that objects have resonant frequencies, and that sound energy can set them vibrating at those frequencies. In the first case, it is the object that's resonating, and in the second, it's the room itself that's resonating.

How might we use this idea, and the principles that underlie it, to illuminate our question about what it means to declare a possibility in a manner that actually allows that possibility to become manifest in our individual experience? If we use the metaphor of the TV that renders an electrical signal, we have to 'tune' ourselves to that possibility so that we resonate with it. How do we do that?

Notice, first, that we no longer have to do anything about tuning ourselves to the default, already existing possibility. We did that early in life by listening to and watching our elders and our peers and by incorporating their story into the one we tell about ourselves. In other words, we already resonate with the possibility—and the set of options it implies—into which we were born. What we're asking now is how to tune ourselves to a possibility that isn't the one we were born into but that somehow calls to us. The answer relies on a crucial realization. What separates us from this new possibility is *not* that it doesn't exist.

It's already 'in the cable,' so to speak. In terms of the explanation I'm proposing, the barrier between ourselves and a greater range of possibilities of experience is a contradictory belief, *a filter that removes those possibilities*. It's some generalization of one or more of those self-limiting sayings, such as Murphy's Law, or 'This is a terrible economic environment,' or 'There's too much competition,' or 'There's just not enough to go around,' or 'I'm just not worthy of that.' Suppose you were to accept that you are in fact an extension of pure creative energy, and that 'who you really are,' your Self[3], knows this beyond any shred of doubt. In terms of *that* interpretation, the barrier between you and your experience of a new possibility is the failure to realize that those limiting statements, which everybody 'knows' to be true, are not actually true!

What is a belief?

Let's inquire into the nature of belief, and into the relationship between beliefs and thoughts. The dictionary defines belief as "confidence in the truth or existence of something not immediately susceptible to rigorous proof." For many people, a belief in God is an example. But what about 'We live in a challenging economic climate'? That idea qualifies as a belief,

---

[3] This is the first time I have capitalized the word Self. This Self is our Being, not something that we have.

but it doesn't fit the dictionary definition, which requires that it not be immediately susceptible to rigorous proof. If you believe that you live in tough economic times, you will see corroborating evidence everywhere, which you would then consider proof of your belief.

I would argue that the dictionary definition of the word 'belief' is part of the old cosmology. In the old cosmology, the world is real, we have no choice but to deal with it as it is, and our beliefs simply represent our best efforts at classifying and organizing whatever we recognize to be true.

As part of our effort to understand what a new cosmology might entail, we need a new definition of 'belief.' I like to think of it this way: a belief is a particular combination of thoughts that have been declared repeatedly and long enough that they become both self-evident and self-fulfilling. An example of that kind of belief is, 'My experience of financial abundance depends most directly on the state of the economy.' It's something that everybody 'knows,' and if you hear it enough times, you come to take it for granted, whereupon you see evidence for its validity everywhere. If you believe that you live in tough economic times, you really have no choice but to act as if your belief is true.

In this frame of reference, beliefs are self-fulfilling. They act as filters, excluding all thoughts that don't conform to the belief in question and allowing only those thoughts that are consistent with it. So, the relationship between beliefs and thoughts is that of context and content. Establish the context, the belief, and the content, or thoughts, will conform to and continually validate the belief.

Werner Erhard spoke of a vicious circle, wherein our beliefs determine our experiences, our experiences confirm and validate our beliefs, which serve to further determine our experiences, which more fully validate our beliefs, and so on. That idea is entirely consistent with an alternative way of looking at things, in which what we call the world is actually an interpretation or description rather than the world itself. If you were to accept that we literally create the world through interpretation, then it would be easier to accept that our beliefs dictate the terms of that interpretation.

Superstitions

The Merriam-Webster dictionary defines superstition as "a belief or practice resulting from ignorance, fear of the unknown, ... or a false conception of causation." Most of us would agree that 'black cats are bad luck' is a superstition. There may well be people who believe, or once believed, that black cats are actually bad luck. Yet any such ominous significance of black cats isn't based on reason or knowledge, and most of us would agree that fear of black cats would be based on a misunderstanding of causation. Furthermore, superstitions only have power when they're not perceived to be superstitions, but rather when they're perceived to be real, part of 'the way it is.'

So how about this statement: 'It's hard to find a good job in this economy.' Is that real, or is that a superstition? Again, if you believe in the truth of that statement about good jobs being hard to find in this economy, then you don't see it as a superstition. You see it as truth, as being *real*. It will then determine not only your actions but your experience as well. However, if you believe that the statement is itself a superstition, then it is not likely to change your actions, and it may not even affect your experience. You simply accept that many people believe it, just as there are people who believe that black cats are bad luck.

There are those among us who experience both prosperity and personal freedom on a daily basis. As a rather obvious example, I occasionally drive up to Aspen and pass the airport with its usual array of private jets parked right next to the highway. Clearly, there are people for whom prosperity and personal freedom coexist in harmony as a distinct possibility. As we all know, there are people who thrive in every difficult economy, just as there are people who struggle in every good economy.

If you want to explain to yourself why those 'lucky' folks have options the rest of us don't, and you're not satisfied with 'luck' or 'circumstances of birth' or even 'incredibly hard work' as possible reasons, I'll offer another possibility. They believe in a different set of 'causal abstractions.' They hold beliefs that don't limit, or filter out, those options. Their 'film strips' don't block those metaphorical frequencies of light, and the possibilities they represent, from appearing on the screen of life.

How *do* our beliefs determine our experience?

In the old cosmology, the old explanation for why things are as they are, things just *are* the way they are, and our beliefs about those 'things' are either true or they're not. According to that view, if we want to change the way things are, all we can do is try to make those changes through action. And furthermore, our beliefs have almost nothing to do with changing our situation.

If we believe that we live in a difficult economy, that there is only so much to go around, and that good jobs are scarce, then we will be inclined to interpret every experience, and everything other people say about this topic, in that light. If someone speaks about his efforts to obtain a job, we see that effort as a struggle. And to people who already have good jobs (or private jets), we say they're just lucky, or they just happened to be in the right place at the right time.

Let's now inquire into the relationship between belief and experience in a 'new cosmology,' in the context of an explanation wherein the world we experience is a description of the world based on interpretation and not some fixed, concrete world external to ourselves.

If we look at life from there, we can learn to tell a different story about our lives; we can make a new 'film strip.' We can come to see that a job, the work performed, and the compensation received are actually a function of our hearts' desires, limited only by beliefs that contradict those desires. We can come to see that the possibility we live in contains a variety of options sufficient to satisfy those desires, and that it is only by considering some of those options as unavailable that we limit ourselves to those that remain. And finally, we can come to understand that the unavailable options we may wish we had are excluded only by beliefs we have never questioned.

CHAPTER 10

OUR STORIES

The futility of action

At this point, we are beginning to ask about the implications of *living as if what we think of as the world is actually a description which we've accepted as being real.* This is as opposed to living in a world that exists independently of ourselves. What would be the purpose of action given *that* premise?

Let's review. We human beings believe that the conditions in which we find ourselves determine our experience. Looking at things from there, a primary purpose of action is to change conditions. This is another of those unexamined assumptions that seems so obvious as to be invisible. Clearly, we human beings use action to fix things that are broken, to make things happen, to change our experience, and hopefully that of others, for the better.

However, now we are exploring the possibility that we are interpreting sensory stimuli according to a description that we've already accepted as real and which thus functions as a filter. This filter allows only those perceptions that confirm and validate what we already know about the world. In our film metaphor, the film in the projector functions as a filter, allowing only the necessary frequencies of light to pass through it and combine to form the world depicted in the movie.

We already looked at the idea that any description that we believe in carries within it a certain, limited range of options. Suppose again that I describe myself as unworthy of experiencing true financial abundance. That description carries within it the options called, 'Keep this job because you may not find a better one' and 'Get a different job because anything's got to be better than this,' or something of that nature. That set of options doesn't include a story such as 'All you have to do is follow your heart and your passion.'

This latter story can be expanded to read, 'If you follow your passion you will wind up inventing, writing, or otherwise creating something that other people will find valuable or useful. You will do it because it feels good to do it, and abundance will follow.' There are people who believe in this possibility and who find it manifested in their experience. But that possibility is not available if you consider yourself unworthy of it. The filtering principle I spoke of implies that however much action you engage in, you can at best only trade one limited option for another one, all within the range of options dictated by the description you have accepted as being *real*.

Ok, what would the purpose of action be in a world that mirrors your description of it? Since the conditions you encounter are simply reflecting your description of the world, the world itself doesn't need to be fixed. The same is true of the content of your life experience.

If you accept that proposition, then what remains as a purpose of acting in the world? What remains is to act for the enjoyment of being in action, to revel in the sights and sounds of the world, to love being and interacting with other people, and so on. In other words, in this alternative interpretation of reality, we really can act simply for the joy of it. This flies in the face of so many cultural dictates we can barely hear it. But it is enormously freeing if you can come to realize, or make real for yourself, that nothing in our lives is broken, and nothing in our lives needs to be fixed.

In terms of this new explanation, everything we experience is an accurate rendering of our view of the world and our view of ourselves. Having a world of experience that shows up as a reflection of our view of the world is what I call a reflexive world. It behaves exactly like a mirror.

What's "out there" is simply a reflection of what's "in here."

A REFLEXIVE INTERPRETATION OF THE WORLD WE EXPERIENCE

If the world we experience constitutes a reflection of our beliefs, then the purpose of the world can be said to allow us to see ourselves. In mundane terms, a reflection is useful when shaving or combing one's hair, for example. If you look at it that way, trying to change situations or conditions solely with action in the world would be like trying to fix an unwanted image in the mirror without changing what's being reflected. It just doesn't work.

Here is an admittedly absurd but telling example. Imagine that you get up in the morning, go into the bathroom, and look at yourself in the mirror. There's a gigantic pimple right in the middle of your forehead! That won't do – you have a meeting this morning with an important person and you have a date tonight! So, you get out your container of makeup, climb up on the bathroom counter so you can see really well, and you carefully apply makeup to cover up the pimple – onto your image in the mirror. Well, you haven't really changed anything, have you? And yet, if we live in an interpretation-based world in which the world faithfully reflects back to us who we've been considering ourselves to be, that's exactly what we do when we try to fix what we think is broken in the circumstances of our lives!

A personal battle for power

Allow me to indulge in some personal reflections here to underscore the possibilities that become available when you change your story, when you learn to relate to the world differently.

I venture to say that everyone who knew me and my parents when I was growing up saw a loving, fully functional family unit. That was my experience much of the time. Underneath the surface, however, there were dynamics at play that would have required a dispassionate and careful viewing to perceive. Recognition of these dynamics in my later life have served me as a way to illuminate the idea of a reflexive world of experience.

My mother was certainly the dominant figure in much of my life. She and I were on the planet together for about sixty-two years. Memories and photos that I have from our early years together show us to have been especially close. My father died around the time of my high school graduation, so my relationship with my mother became the dominant influence in my life.

During my academic years, my mother was fully supportive of my path in life. I never thought much about that support; I just assumed it was a natural part of my emotional landscape. When I left school for street politics, and later for playing music in Aspen, I felt her approval steadily diminish. I fought hard to get it back. I kept her apprised of my efforts to make my own way, and I consistently attempted to regain that approval by explaining why I made the choices I did. However, in 1970, playing folk, rock, and country music in Aspen, Colorado, I had seemingly left behind an important, and certainly not inexpensive, education and career path. I expended enormous quantities of energy trying to justify myself to Mom.

I didn't realize at the time what was really going on. I was not aware that I was engaged in a power struggle that largely defined my being in the world. Throughout my childhood, I believed that personal power was 'out there,' principally in the hands of my parents. Much later, I came to see that for many decades the defining theme of my life was to try to get that power back. I made choices that made me happy, and then I tried, mostly unsuccessfully, to get my mother to agree that they were the 'right' choices.

I also came to understand that what I had previously seen as a struggle to be right in a disagreement with someone 'out there' was better understood as a conflict within myself. Over many decades I had internalized my mother's view of a son's proper behavior, and that view conflicted with the choices I was making. Not understanding that point, I projected the conflict outwards into my relationship with her. From that perspective, my mother never accepted me for who I am.

—〰—

I have just related a story about a mother and a son. It has elements that many readers might find to be similar to their own stories. 'She just doesn't understand me. My life would be so much better if she did!' That's the story I invented. I fed it from year to year, and for me that story *was* the relationship. After her passing, however, something different happened that relates directly to the new life story, the new explanation I've been trying to explain in this work.

The 'Petty Tyrant'

In the course of many, many hours of reflection on that relationship, I've come to see what Werner Erhard meant when he spoke of the vicious circle, where our beliefs determine our experiences, and our experiences confirm and validate our beliefs. I realize now that the story I told all those years about my relationship with my mother not only served to justify my actions and feelings but also served to perpetuate the 'difficulty' of the relationship, the power struggle I couldn't win and didn't even manage to identify as such.

As time went by, after my mother passed, I sought a 'better' answer, a more satisfying and empowering way to think about our relationship. I was reminded of yet another idea I took from Juan Matus, the idea of the petty tyrant. According to Castaneda, Matus said that the world itself is the Tyrant, because its reflection back to us of the description into which we live our lives is inexorable and unyielding. From that point of view, there seems to be no getting around the fact that whatever story we tell gets reflected back to us, and the conditions of our lives will not change until we tell a different story.

Compared to the Tyrant, that inescapable reflection, the persistence of the people in our lives who hound us is almost insignificant, and so in Castaneda's telling these people are called 'petty tyrants.' Actually, you could say these petty tyrants are the personification of the Universe in a form that we can relate to as human beings.[4]

Anyway, back to that story I told for so many years about Mom and me. I continued to tell it to other people for a while after she passed, but it felt increasingly uncomfortable to do so. Finally, there came a moment when I realized that to move beyond my feelings of resentment and anger toward her, I had to tell a different story. So, I decided to say to people that she had actually made a significant contribution to my search for understanding of what a human being really is, the inquiry that is the subject of this book. Without any hope of feeling the satisfaction I thought I would gain from convincing her that I was on the 'right' path, I had no choice but to go deeper into the understanding of who I really am so that I could feel *real* certainty. Therefore, I made her my petty tyrant, my life coach, after the fact.

That choice bore fruit in several different ways. Whereas prior to her passing, our relationship had become a struggle, I

---

[4] You may have noticed that I have begun to capitalize the word 'Universe.' That's because I now know it to be alive, aware of me, willing and eager to lead me to a deeper understanding of my essential nature, the ultimate expression of who I really am.

now no longer felt the distress of its decline. I began to think and speak of her with love again, without the guilt one might expect to feel from a difficult end to a relationship with a parent. And second, feeling all right with her again seems to have opened up the possibility of getting these ideas down 'on paper.'

I always felt powerless with respect to my mother, and that made me feel powerless in general. I realize now that large portions of my behavior patterns as an adult are simply continuations of childhood efforts to regain my power by resisting hers. I remember the dictates of Newton's Third Law of Motion, which is that what you push against tends to push back. In terms of one's life, that law becomes 'what you resist persists.' I am no longer pushing against Mom, and I can feel the freedom that comes from relinquishing that particular addiction.

Recontextualization of others

The shift from tormentor to relentless teacher is an example of what Erhard called 'recontextualization.' Recontextualization means you don't change the circumstance; you just change the context in which you put the circumstance. I find that it works with memories, relationships, current conditions, and anything else that feels bad when I think about it. Recontextualizing my adult relationship with my mother didn't change any of our history. But it turned her from a tormentor into a life coach, the kind of coach who recognizes your potential on the playing field and won't leave you alone until you realize that potential.

The best part of all this is that I now feel my power returning. I can feel my power, my ability to live the way I want to live, to be who I am, without trying to please others. I can feel my power to express myself honestly, to be who I am in the world just for the sake of being who I am. And I can almost feel my mother 'on the other side,' cheering me on.

A couple of weeks after she passed, I had a dream about her. In the dream she appeared to me as a little girl, dressed in a little white dress with a bow in her hair, much as she appears in an old photograph. As she walked across my field of view, she smiled at me and said she was 'off to school.' I awoke from the dream with certainty that she was letting me know she was off to meet with her spiritual guides; they would help her consider the lifetime she had just lived and the lessons to be gained from it. And now the recontextualization of my mother is largely complete. I see her as having chosen to be here with me all these years, to serve as my life coach, the type of coach who will not let you alone until you realize your potential.

Believing in a new story

It seems clear to me that to change our lives we must change the story we tell about our lives. That is equivalent to replacing the film in our metaphorical projector with a new one. In our lives, however, that's tricky. If we tell a story that reflects the life we want, but we don't believe it can be true, it won't feel good, and it won't change our lives.

Once again, let's say we feel we don't have enough money. Perhaps that is because we've been telling a story for a long time that paints us as victims of economic circumstances, or of insufficient education, or of too much wealth concentrated in the hands of too few. Or maybe it is because we decided long ago that we could rationalize not having much money by considering ourselves as being 'more spiritual,' or by saying that 'money is the root of all evil.' Telling those kinds of stories might in the short run make us feel better, but they don't change anything, which reinforces our feeling of powerlessness with respect to money, and that doesn't feel good at all. It has been said that in life, you either have what you want or the reasons why not.

On the other hand, suddenly telling a story in which we have plenty of money won't feel good either, because we know we don't believe it, and every time we look at our bank balances, we feel the same powerlessness all over again. So, then, are we left with a slow, incremental approach to changing our ideas about ourselves, and about what is really possible for us, or is there some form of leverage available with which we can change those ideas in larger chunks?

Let's look at a metaphor that may shed some light on why it seems so difficult to change the story we tell about our lives, and that may provide a way to get a bit more leverage.

If you were to finish your bathroom floor by laying large tiles on top of flooring that's not perfectly level, every time you walk on it, the tiles will shift. As a result, the grout that you so carefully spread between the tiles will crack and come out, and you will have to keep replacing it. I know this from experience! It's the underlying floor that's the problem.

Similarly, if you have a belief system that rests on top of a core belief that you never examine, it is really hard to alter your 'thought universe' because any new thoughts that conflict with that core belief won't be stable; they won't become new habits of thought. The stories we tell about our lives are built from, and are consistent with, our thought universe. So, to change our thought universe we have to begin to change our core beliefs. Well, how do we do *that*?

CHAPTER 11

HOW CAN WE CHANGE OUR CORE BELIEFS?

Getting unstuck from superstitions

As I wrestled with this question about changing my thoughts, searching for core beliefs that seemed to keep me stuck in old patterns, I remembered moments during my scientific studies when shifting my perspective made understanding certain principles much easier. As I thought about this, I realized that modern physics had offered me powerful examples of how getting unstuck from unexamined assumptions can open up an entire field of new possibilities.

A classic example of such an opening was the transition from a geocentric, earth-centered view of our planetary neighborhood to a heliocentric, sun-centered view. I referred to this shift earlier in connection with looking at the tenacity with which we hold onto our beliefs. This time the context is the power afforded us in recognizing and relinquishing mistaken beliefs.

It goes without saying that we live in a technological age. Some, though certainly not all, of the world's population benefits enormously from material advances that would have been literally unthinkable without an increasingly improved scientific understanding of how the world works. I strongly suspect that each of the technological advances we now take for granted came about because we humans freed ourselves from some superstition that had previously held sway.

I could easily argue that one of our era's most useful technologies, the global positioning system or GPS, came into being as a possibility when our then-common understanding got unstuck from the idea that everything visible in the sky goes around the earth. Prior to the age of Copernicus and Galileo, everybody accepted this geocentric interpretation. Everybody *knew* that the earth was the center of the universe. But GPS and many other aspects of modern communications depend on satellites launched into orbits. And these orbits could not have been calculated, much less achieved, without Newton's theory of gravity. And that theory, in turn, would have been literally unthinkable without the understanding that the sun, not the earth, is the center of the solar system.

It may be that the most consequential superstition embedded in our belief systems is the assumption that we are temporary visitors in a universe that's permanent. We are convinced that the physical world is senior to us, in that it exists much as it appears to us, whether or not there is anyone or anything around to perceive it. My study of modern physics has convinced me that this proposition is patently false. Our ability to explain what we are likely to see when we undertake an experiment on the physical world was greatly enhanced when we got unstuck from the idea that *there has to be a way the world really is when we're not looking at it.* From a scientific perspective, this is our fundamental superstition.

The enigma of quantum physics

Quantum physics presents us with an enigma that has persisted for over one hundred years. When you really examine the powerful theory of quantum mechanics, you realize that it gives you the probability of *observing* any particular configuration of the physical world. It is completely silent on the way the world 'really' is when nobody is actually observing it. In technical terms, it tells you only what the *likelihood* is of an experiment yielding any particular result out of a distribution of possible results.

However, in making some physical measurement, one *does* find one specific answer, and in making that measurement, we do not experience the uncertainty inherent in a distribution of many possibilities. How does that happen? How does the world 'know' which of its possible configurations to pick during an observation? Attempts to answer that question have resulted in several 'interpretations of quantum mechanics.' And it turns out that there are a couple of ways to think about quantum theory that are consistent with what I call the seer's explanation, a radically different idea of our relationship to the world around us. They are referred to as the 'Many-Worlds' and the 'QBist' approaches. I'll summarize them.

The Many-Worlds approach to quantum physics

The equations of quantum theory describe mathematically a distribution of probable results of any experiment that *is yet to be performed* on a system of fundamental, exceedingly small particles. Those equations then describe how that distribution of experimental results will vary over time. This process is known as the propagation of probability waves.

In 1956, a physicist named Hugh Everett came up with an interpretation of quantum mechanics called the Many-Worlds Approach. Everett said that "a more careful reading of Schrodinger's math leads somewhere else [than one and only one reality]: to a plentiful reality populated by an ever-growing collection of universes."

Erwin Schrodinger was the physicist who discovered the equation that correctly describes how the probability waves propagate. Given the way any small piece of the world looks in this moment, the equation describes the probability that it will look any particular way in a future moment. Everett's idea is that, rather than the range of probable outcomes collapsing into the 'real' answer, such as to the question of one electron's location, all the possibilities are actually represented in different 'universes.' He further proposes that none of these 'universes' are actually more real than the others.

Now, we human beings only perceive one universe. So, *where are these other universes?* Where are the alternate universes that correspond to different outcomes of measurements whose statistical likelihood are predicted by the probability waves? Furthermore, why don't we usually *perceive* them?

Notice that questions that begin with 'where' imply a static, ultimate-context concept of space, the one we are taught when we're young. This concept is the one in which space is the ultimate container of everything else, and every object large and small has a particular location in space.

To clarify this idea, think of your house as the container of all your stuff. Then you could ask, "Where is that thing I misplaced?" and that question would make perfect sense. Normally, we take for granted the interpretation of space (and time) as the context for everything else. If we think of all the possible quantum mechanical universes as taking place within a static idea of space and time, we get science fiction stories in which 'wormholes,' say, take us from one world to another.

However, you can consider the possibility that space and time are themselves *components of the description of the world we have learned to perceive.* What is the answer to the question, 'Where are these other universes,' in that case? In human *experience*, there is only one answer to the question 'where is it?' and that answer is 'here.' After all, a human being can only experience 'here' and 'now.' 'There' and 'then' are completely different ideas; they are ultimately components of memory, and they can never be directly experienced.

In terms of this understanding, all possibilities for the configuration of the physical universe are actually present here and now. Our perception of only one of them is the result of how we focus our attention. Essentially, we ignore all the other configurations this unimaginably large system could take on, and we focus on one possibility alone. In other words, we filter out all the other possible actualizations of the so-called 'probability waves' that our learned description of the world does not allow.

so many frequencies

LIKE A TV THAT RECEIVES MANY CHANNELS AT ONCE

None is visible until one is selected

ACCORDING TO QUANTUM PHYSICS, THE WORLD IS A MATHEMATICAL DESCRIPTION OF POSSIBLE REALITIES

One way to think about all these possible realities being here and now is to remember that all the television channels—and thus all the television programs—that are currently available are all 'here' and 'now' as far as the TV is concerned. In essence, they are all in the same location in space and time—in the cable, right now. Our ability to distinguish one from another so we can watch a particular program is a matter of how we tune the TV.

Is it possible to enter one of those other worlds and observe an outcome different from the one that appears so real? Again, a science-fiction enthusiast would have a field day with that question, no doubt involving some sophisticated machine with a dial on it that allows you to select one of the other worlds. However, there is a much simpler possibility: we do it all the time!

I suggest that we *do* enter the alternative worlds Everett spoke of. That is to say, I suggest we *do* perceive alternate vibrational configurations that are just as real as the one we're accustomed to perceiving. Most of those 'other worlds' are quite similar to one another, even though we think the world we currently perceive is the only world there is. Let me use the television metaphor again to illustrate this.

On the TV set I had when I was in high school, there was a fine-tuning knob that allowed me to perform very subtle adjustments to the gross tuning mechanism of the channel selector. Some folks will remember adjusting the rabbit-ears on top of the television! Doing so helped get rid of the 'snow' that often appeared on the screen. It's that metaphorical fine-tuning I'm speaking of here. In our lives, we adjust our precise vibrational configuration as our mood, our feelings, and our expectations change during the day, and for most of us this tends to happen in response to life's conditions.

When we adjust our vibrations like that, we might just make the traffic light we otherwise would have missed, or we might happen to run into a particular person who otherwise might have just left by the time we arrived. The experience of timing (as in 'good timing!') is one of the hallmarks of the shift from one of Everett's many worlds to another.

The QBist approach to quantum physics

The second of those two interpretations of quantum mechanics, to which I referred earlier, is called the QBist approach. Don't let the name fool you ... it has nothing to do with art! However, I believe it is an even better match to the seer's explanation. It says that those possible arrangements of the world predicted by quantum theory represent the degree of belief an observer has about each possible outcome of measurements. In other words, the likelihood of the world appearing to us in any particular form is a function of the strength of our belief that it will actually appear that way.

The laws of quantum physics speak to our perception and not to any external reality. And this is totally consistent with the seer's explanation, which says that perception is not about our observations of some external reality. The QBist approach to quantum physics says, instead, that the reality we perceive is ultimately a function of which reality we believe will show up.

It might help to visualize that each fundamental particle (the protons, neutrons, and electrons that make up ordinary stuff) has some possibility of being observed at every point in space, as implied by the mathematics of quantum mechanics. If you extend that idea to every particle that makes up what we conceive of as the world, every particle is then to some degree everywhere. In that light, it seems a bit less outlandish that we could see a slightly different configuration of physical objects and events than the one we're presently observing, based on our state of mind.

How assumptions constrain perception

It is well established that observation is *the* critical factor in causing our physical world to appear the way it does. And for us humans, observation is really about perception.

What does it mean that, for us humans, observation is really about perception? Let's explore those two distinctions, observation and perception. To a physicist, 'observation' is a technical term, meaning that the collection of particles making up what is being observed comes into contact with another collection of particles, namely those making up the human and his or her measuring equipment. 'Perception' is different.

In terms of the traditional explanation for the world, perception is "the process of using the senses to acquire information about the surrounding environment." In terms of my proposed alternative explanation for the world, the surrounding environment is in reality a conditioned interpretation of sensory input. In that context, perception is the process of using our description of the world to filter and interpret the complex vibrational signal to which we're tuned in order to render a stable, coherent, multi-sensory *picture* of the world.

The point here is that *the alternative definition of 'human being' that I am proposing is entirely consistent with quantum physics.* We are fluid beings, capable of perceiving a multiplicity of realities. All possible configurations of the world that have ever been imagined actually exist in this moment, right here and now, and the one we're experiencing right now is the one to which we are an emotional match.

When we shift from one of those possible worlds to another by virtue of a shift in our emotional state, the change is seamless for everybody else's reality. That's because the Universe, All-That-Is, non-physical conscious energy, arranges each and every human being's experience as a perfect, effortless composite of those emotional states. In this view, our emotional state is the fine-tuning knob I spoke of earlier, the one that gets rid of the 'snow' on the TV screen and allows the picture to be sharper and more true to life.

CHAPTER 12

HOW CAN WE CHANGE OUR EMOTIONAL UNIVERSE?

The emotional 'set-point'

In the last chapter, we touched upon the notion that our emotional state is the fine-tuning knob with which we can make subtle adjustments in our perception of the world. To obtain a deeper understanding of this idea, let's look at the nature and scope of the emotional landscape upon which we are making these adjustments.

In their book, *Ask and It Is Given,* Esther and Jerry Hicks propose just such an emotional scale.[5] It ranges from joy (and the related states of freedom and love) at the upper end, to fear (and despair and powerlessness) at the lower end. In between those two poles, they list twenty gradations, including passion, hopefulness, doubt, and jealousy. This scale represents discrete jumps in our emotional well-being, though one could just as well portray it as a continuous range.

---

[5] Esther and Jerry Hicks, *Ask and It Is Given* (New York: Hay House, 2004), 114.

While most of us find our emotions fluctuating during the course of each day, all of my personal influencers referred in one way or another to a 'set point' about which those fluctuations take place. To visualize this set point, you can think of average seasonal variations in temperature, about which daily temperatures fluctuate from day to day. Let's look at how this average emotional 'temperature' is correlated with the events and conditions, the circumstances of our lives.

The emotional temperature and our reality

From a typical person's point of view, this correlation may seem obvious. Most people believe that their emotional temperature is a product of the events and conditions they encounter. However, my argument is that in reality it works the other way around. Your emotional temperature determines the quality of the events and conditions of your life, and you can *feel* the correlation between those two domains.

At this point, you may well ask, 'Ok, how do I access the fine-tuning knob that I can use to adjust my emotional state?' Quantum physics implies that we can select a different world from the 'Many-Worlds,' or from the expectations inherent in the QBist approach. But how does it work in the real world, in our daily lives?

The shamans and the quantum physicists

To see how fine-tuning works in our daily lives, we must step back a bit for a broader view of our thoughts and beliefs. Let's start with our understanding of time. We humans have been trained since birth to regard our lives as a linear sequence of events. This view is reflected in our memories, which are arranged according to successive moments of 'now.' It is also reflected in our universal assumption, which goes mostly unnoticed, that time and space are fixed containers in which our lives take place. It is worthwhile, however, to further examine what happens if we think of time and space as components of the *description* of our lives and of the world, and not fundamental aspects of the world itself.

Both interpretations of quantum mechanics I included in the previous chapter can be useful in dealing with the quantum enigma (how we get from a field of possible realities to the one we experience in each moment). Yet they are typically considered by people who assume that time and space form the context *in which* consciousness arose as an attribute of our species—and perhaps other species, such as whales and dolphins and chimpanzees. I questioned that assumption as I began this book, and I proposed instead that we think of consciousness as the context *which gives rise to* time, space, and all the other ideas we think of as being part of the world.

If we look at our lives in terms of that proposition, and we remember that *experientially*, 'now' is all there is, I believe we can see that our notion of time is a mental construct. It is *we* who arrange memories in a linear fashion, whereas the events they record, in a deep sense, take place *simultaneously, in an ever-present 'now.'* The same argument can be made about all the objects in space being 'here,' because 'here' is the only place we can experience them. The question then arises, 'How could we think about alternative realities, or quantum possibilities, from *that* viewpoint?' At first glance, that seems like a real head-scratcher! Let's ask the 'experts' about this.

THE SHAMAN AND THE SCIENTIST

Both the shaman and the physicist have developed explanations about the relationship between abstract possibilities and physical realities. At first glance, it would seem that the world of a shaman and that of the quantum physicist are completely different. Let's see, however, if we can find common ground between the two, and whether that common ground can shed any light on the difficult question in the preceding paragraph.

My first exposure to the world of the shaman was in Castaneda's writings. Juan Matus called himself a sorcerer, but later writers have referred to him as a shaman. More recently, I came upon Jose Stevens, the co-founder of Power Path Seminars, a firm dedicated to "the study of shamanism and indigenous wisdom." I was fascinated to discover that Matus and Stevens referenced a common language, a language that includes the term 'assemblage point.'

Juan Matus said that our experience of the world is determined by something he called the 'position of the assemblage point.' In terms of his explanation, all sentient creatures have an assemblage point that selects specific vibrational frequencies for emphasis, and it is with this selection of frequencies that we assemble the world we perceive. Furthermore, by selecting a different set of frequencies, the world we perceive shifts and actually becomes, to some degree, a different world.

Jose Stevens speaks about the idea of the assemblage point as follows:

> Each creature whether plant, animal, or human has an assemblage point located somewhere in its energetic field. This assemblage point could be described as a kind of computer chip or bar code that contains highly condensed information about the identity of the product in the package, its date and whereabouts of manufacture, its shipping history, its price and so on. In the case of a human being this is a kind of ID that states where this soul has been, what they have learned thus far, what they know and are aware of, where they are headed, who they think they are now in the context of a gender, a culture, a race, a profession, what their current personality traits are, their karma, their agreements, what is in their script for this life, what their intentions are, and what their current choices are. Bear in mind that a good part of this information is subject to change based on choices made.[6]

According to Juan Matus, for most human beings the position of that assemblage point remains fixed during the

---

[6] Jose Stevens, https://thepowerpath.com/articles-by-jose-stevens/article-one-understanding-big-picture-state-affairs-usa-world/

person's entire lifetime. Yet he said it can be made, or rather allowed, to shift. In fact, with the silencing of what he called the 'internal dialog,' it will shift naturally to a new position in which one experiences a more effortless, accepting, and more joyful view of the world. And according to Matus, the ability to purposely allow that point of emphasis to undergo a profound shift is what makes the person a sorcerer.

If the shift of the assemblage point is subtle, new possibilities can be perceived, and new abilities can emerge. If the shift is profound, the world we know can be made to disappear altogether, and a substantially different world can be assembled. In quantum terms, this is equivalent to proposing that by changing which of the possible configurations of the world he or she focusses on, an observer can alter the way the world shows up in his or her experience, possibly to a profound degree.

It seems to me that in each of these shamanistic references, the assemblage point is equivalent to the quantum mechanical likelihood that any particular arrangement of the world will be observed. In terms of the Many-Worlds approach, that likelihood is a function of which world we tune ourselves to, using the 'fine-tuning knob' of our emotions to determine the position of our assemblage point. In the case of the QBism approach, the probability of making a particular observation is dependent on the observer tuning his or her assemblage point by altering the degree to which he or she believes in that specific possibility.

Carlos Castaneda recounts suddenly recalling episodes in which he encounters people in Matus's world who did not exist in his memory prior to that remembrance. It is particularly striking to me that those experiences seemed to him to occur 'out of time,' outside the linear sequence we all believe in. It seemed that Castaneda, under the influence of a 'sorcerer,' moved his assemblage point to a new position, wherein he was temporarily in a different time and place with people he simply could not encounter in his normal state of awareness.

At first blush, this possibility seems a flight of fancy, if a clever and moving one. Yet it seems to me entirely consistent with both the 'Many-Worlds' and the 'QBist' approach to quantum mechanics. Each of those explanations denies the idea of a fixed reality and instead proposes a multitude of possible realities. Furthermore, when we include my proposition that when we talk about a reality, we're actually talking about a *description* of the world, time and space can show up differently because those descriptions include the manner in which time and space present themselves.

I should say that in my world, the probability of meeting up with a sorcerer (as defined by Juan Matus), or of demonstrably assembling a substantially different reality, feels remote. But perhaps it only feels that way because of the constant barrage of messages from every possible direction that the world is the way everybody 'knows' it is. In other words, those other possibilities are not gone; they're like TV stations that are not currently being tuned in because we have been convinced that they don't exist.

Esther Hicks, speaking as Abraham, tells a story about Hicks searching in vain for a particularly special pen. As most of us have experienced, searching for something special and not finding it is often accompanied by feelings of frustration, anger, or fear. The story has Hicks searching every purse, bag, drawer, and every other conceivable place before just giving up, resigned to the apparent fact that the pen was lost. Finally, days or weeks later, when she had completely forgotten the effort and was focused on other things, she put her hand in a particular purse (which she had previously searched thoroughly, turned upside down, and so on) and came out with the pen. A traditional explanation would be that before she found it, she somehow just missed it. But what if, by relaxing and being at peace with the pen's absence, she allowed her assemblage point to move ever so slightly to a position that also contained the pen's vibrational frequency? Just saying ...

In my life I have observed, through the practice of quieting the internal dialog, the noise dying down and other possibilities becoming visible. Again, referring to my story about the gas tank, I believe that in asking the Universe for help and actually getting an audible answer, I was able to surrender or relinquish the problem and allow the noise to die down, whereupon a completely unexpected possibility showed up. This possibility is one that is simply not explicable by the laws of classical physics or, for that matter, by common sense.

However, different realities *are* allowed by quantum laws, and I believe that my experience was manifested by a power consistent with those laws. That power is in accord with Juan Matus's description of the Nagual, and I am left with the certainty that it lies within me, within all of us. This possibility, that you can create your own reality, consigns all apparent constraints on your thought universe to the category of superstition.

Clearly, the possibility I have just proposed is in sharp contrast to the one we inherited from our culture. In order for us to experience it, we have to declare it in what Werner Erhard called an 'act of existential courage.' We must give our entire being to that possibility. And in so doing, we can gain control over the quality of our lives and, in the process, glimpse what a human being really is: a creator of worlds.

CHAPTER 13

WHO OR WHAT DETERMINES QUALITY OF LIFE?

Measuring the quality of life

Thus far, I have offered an alternative view of the world around us and of our place in it. I have suggested that we can choose to regard the world as an interpretation of information provided by our senses, as opposed to a durable, external entity that will outlast us. This new view offers us a choice of how to look at our lives.

Apart from what everybody 'knows' about that choice, how might we decide which of those explanations to use in our daily lives? I suggest that the only value of an explanation about who and what we are, and what the world really is, has to involve the quality of one's life. In other words, rather than being 'true,' an explanation about who you are, and what the world is, has to be useful to *you*. It must work in the area of your quality of life.

How are we to measure the quality of life? It seems obvious to me each of us can only measure the quality of one human life, and that is our own. As well as I think I know other people, I sense deep down that I don't really know much about their paths through life, or what their purposes are in being here. That limitation has left me in a considerable state of bewilderment, and not in just a few cases. 'Why did she say that?' 'Why is he acting that way?' Those questions seem to lead inevitably to asking myself what I did wrong, or to ask, 'How can I alter my actions or words so that I elicit from her or him behavior and words that feel better to me? How can I be better?'

There's no logical way out of that mess of self-criticism. Like most everyone else, I grew up believing that other peoples' actions and words have power when it comes to the quality of my life, when it comes to how I really feel. When you look at other people from there, from thinking that they affect your happiness, you can't see them as who they really are, but rather only as others whom you have to manipulate or with whom you have to contend.

When I think about measuring the quality of my own life, however, things become quite clear. I know when I feel good about my life, and I know when I don't. For me, happiness is intimately related to peacefulness. If I'm at peace with the way things are, what I really am is happy. That's what has allowed me to relinquish my addiction to emotions such as 'thrill' as a counterbalance to disappointment and resignation.

In my experience, that's the whole point of quieting the internal dialog. In the practice of meditation, for example, thoughts diminish by degrees, only to arise again when attention wavers, only to be released again when one becomes aware that one's attention has wavered, and so on. As verbal thought, the internal dialog, dies down, I am left with focusing my attention on just being, on just being aware. In those quiet moments I feel the peace I refer to. However, I've found I can also experience that peace whenever I maintain focus on an actual in-the-moment experience, as opposed to thinking about experiences.

I practice doing this while walking, driving, playing music, and being with a good and trusted friend.

To feel the peace I've just described, it seems that thought must diminish. Does that mean that if I want to feel good, I can't have thoughts? Actually, it doesn't mean that at all. In the presence of thought, peace seems to be replaced by feeling either the excitement of certain thoughts or the discomfort of other thoughts. What makes the difference? The thoughts that I associate with excitement, anticipation, or just pure enjoyment are thoughts that are consistent with who I really am, in that they don't have components of limitation, scarcity, inevitability, and so on.

On the other hand, the thoughts I find uncomfortable tend to arise from noticing that something is not as I want it to be and, out of habit, trying to fix the situation using rationality and action. That's like putting makeup on the mirror. So, the way I feel serves as guidance. It's an exceptionally reliable guidance system, as long as my objective is to be happy, or to be who I really am, which is saying the same thing. Ultimately, then, feeling good is like Hansel and Gretel's breadcrumbs, a trail I can follow to guide myself back home.

Another summary so far

We have now fleshed out most of the seer's explanation, this alternative explanation of the Being of human beings. It tells us that *what we think of as the world is a description, an interpretation of our sensory input.* It's essentially a story. What we think of as ourselves, the invented self, the Ego[7], 'I,' is also part of that

---

[7] I realize that the word Ego has a technical meaning in the context of Freudian psychoanalysis. I am not using the word in that manner, but rather I use it to refer to our invented self.

story. Everything we perceive, including our personalities, our bodies, and even space and time, is part of that interpretation. None of that is truly real.

Well, what are we left with? What *is* truly real? I have concluded that what is real is experience. Experience happens in the 'right now moment,' which is distinct from the realms I call interpretation, memory, and so on. Experience is what Being does. We do interpret our experience, but that happens *after* we experience in our present. Feelings happen in the 'right now moment' as well. They're not part of the interpretation we call the world. The way I feel is just the way I feel, and it is the way I experience living in the world.

As I write these words, I am keenly aware that I have, in fact, adopted an explanation that constitutes a radical reinterpretation of the world I experience, and of my relationship to it. I often find myself switching back and forth between this new explanation and the one I grew up with, comparing how I feel when applying each explanation in turn to whatever experiences my life offers.

In the next part of this book, I will explore the effect of looking at life using the seer's explanation as opposed to the one we inherited from our culture. I will describe ways of thinking about life from this perspective, using metaphors derived from everyday experience. Perhaps these metaphors will help you more fully understand the value and usefulness of the seer's explanation. Perhaps they will even help you see the expansion of possibility in your own life as you practice telling a different story about who you are.

CHAPTER 14

WHAT MAKES THE SEER'S EXPLANATION DIFFERENT?

In this book, I am suggesting the consideration of an alternative explanation for the world we see when we open our eyes in the morning. As I've said, we already have an explanation for this world that appears in our experience every morning: we're looking at what's there! The alternative explanation is fundamentally different, and especially so in one critical respect. That essential distinction is that in the seer's explanation, the world that we see is actually a description of the world, a story *about* the world, rather than the world itself.

Another way of looking at this distinction is to say: in terms of the culturally inherited explanation, the context or container of everything that we experience, including ourselves, is the world. In the seer's explanation, that context or container is us, our awareness, our consciousness. *We contain the world in our awareness of it.*

In this chapter, we will begin to look at a wide variety of aspects of daily life from the point of view of this new explanation. When you look at life from any alternative point of view, everything looks different. It turns out that the seer's explanation is about as different from the explanation we were given as young people as you can get. So, it should come as no surprise that when you stand on the seer's explanation and look out at your life, everything you think you know about how life is supposed to work comes into question.

The purpose of a description of the world

Why do we have an explanation at all? It's a good question! When we were little, our parents and others continually described the world as they were teaching us language. As we grew, we took over that task, constantly describing the world to ourselves and to each other. At the same time, our awareness became dominated by language, and language is particularly important to us. It enables us to get what we want and need more quickly, more easily, and more safely than by using pointing, pantomime, or physical force.

We are taught that who we are is contained by the outer boundaries of our bodies. Constantly repeating this story to ourselves reinforces our identification with our bodies, so that everything outside those boundaries becomes something else and not us. We are taught meaning. We learn that actions and appearances have meaning to others and, therefore, they should have meaning to us. We learn right and wrong, good and bad, naughty and nice, and so on. As we master those distinctions, we become more and more adept at getting what we want by pleasing those around us. That behavior is constantly self-reinforced because we usually feel better pleasing others rather than annoying them. And thus, we come to see our story about the world as essential to our happiness.

The purpose of having a description of the world is to provide ourselves with a set of symbols whose meaning we have all agreed upon, so that we can interact with each other. Imagine, upon awakening in the morning, that you are confronted with a stereoscopic visual image of areas of different color and shading but without the identification of those different areas as objects, and you'll get an idea of why we need a description of the world. It's like an overlay. It functions like drawing lines and words on a satellite photo of the earth turns the photo into a map.

Let's take a moment to remind ourselves that a symbol is typically a physical object representing some abstract idea. A symbol might be as straightforward as a red octagon representing 'STOP.' Food, as a symbol, is much more nuanced. It's something to eat, but it also represents caring, solidarity, and love. The day my father died, the dining room table was piled high with edibles. No one could have thought we needed that much food to eat. It was given as a symbol of love and sympathy.

We think of our description of the world, our collection of symbols, as referring to, and being separate from, a real tangible world. We assume that there are two separate things: the world, and our description of the world. However, what would happen if we were to discover that our description is, for all intents and purposes, all there is? If that were to be the case, then *the symbols that constitute our description of the world would effectively turn out to make up the world itself.*

When we were taught our native language, we didn't realize that we were also learning a story about the world, a story about how it works and about how to deal with it effectively. As we grew and became more independent, we internalized that story and began a lifelong process of retelling it to ourselves, often with embellishments and with increasing complexity. In the process, we forgot that the story, the description of the world, is something we learned. We forgot that the description

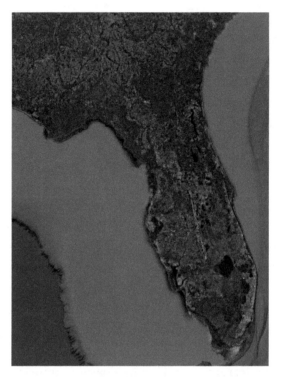

WITHOUT HUMAN BEINGS THERE ARE NO BORDERS

is, in effect, superimposed over our perception of sensory information in the same way that boundaries are superimposed over topological information to create a map.

We all mistake the description of the world for the world itself, and that has profound consequences. It was Werner Erhard who came up with that wonderful metaphor for this confusion. He spoke about the difference between a menu and a meal. I visualize a menu that has mouth-watering photographs of the various dishes. He said (actually, thundered from the stage), "You mistake the menu for the meal! You eat the menu!"

MISTAKING OUR DESCRIPTION OF THE WORLD FOR THE WORLD ITSELF

I venture to say that most of us human beings, to one degree or another, find life unsatisfying. This is especially true in contrast with what we believe it could be or hoped it would be. And so, we cast about for things and people to fill the void, to make us happy, to give us satisfaction. But if we're eating the menu instead of the meal, we won't ever feel satisfied.

Now, what happens when you have billions of people living in a story about the world as if that story is the 'real world'?

Further, what happens when nearly everybody is emotionally committed to their story, so that they feel they have to be 'right' about it? There are billions of us who 'know' deep down that we depend on the manipulation of conditions and circumstances for our happiness. However, we know we can't control those conditions and circumstances, and therefore we feel powerless to affect the quality of our lives. That feeling of powerlessness leaves us with what remains when we lose our power, and that is, essentially, faking it.

I have already suggested the possibility that the world itself is, and will always remain, a mystery. Current scientific efforts to explain strange phenomena such as quantum entanglement, dark energy, and dark matter don't exactly fill me with confidence that these puzzles are close to being solved. Scientists still seem certain that eventually those mysteries will yield to our cherished rationality and reason. However, it could also be that some things are meant to be, and will always remain mysterious, especially for the human mind.

Our commitment to our idea of the world makes us *feel* as if we are powerful, however. We can argue about the world, and we can perhaps win those arguments and bully others into submission [example: politics in the 21st century]. And yet, if we're arguing about a description while believing the disagreement is about some external 'reality,' we may find that winning arguments doesn't empower us in our daily lives. Instead, let's consider what happens if we live with the following understanding of the world: the world itself is recognized as essentially unknowable and is separated from us by the story with which we interpret it.

Choose your own life story

The seer's explanation says that our power as human beings lies in our attention. In a deep sense we are energy, and we direct our energy with the focus of our attention. Whatever we focus upon receives that energy and begins to grow, to expand, and to be amplified into the rich texture of personal experience. However, we don't just direct that attention by selecting phenomena randomly; we use a description, an interpretation, as a way of deciding what to focus upon.

Mostly what we do is focus our attention on what we would like to improve or fix about our lives and the world in general. That's because, in our common interpretation of our lives and of the world, there are huge problems that need to be solved. When a human being lives life from the explanation we inherit from our culture, everything is an 'is.' Life *is* hard, death *is* sad, taxes *are* a burden, suffering *is* inevitable, and so on.

We believe that focusing on those problems is the way to fix them. However, if those problems live in our story about the world, focusing our attention and our energy on those problems just causes them to grow, to expand, and to be amplified into rich texture that we probably don't want!

What if a human being lives life using the seer's explanation? First of all, if you're focusing upon a description of the world, *and you know it's only a description*, you can experiment with changing that description. You realize you don't have to be 'right' about it. As you experiment with this new degree of freedom, you may find that you're not stuck with the world being an 'is.' You may find that shedding the dead weight of inevitability lessens and lightens your load.

Most importantly, for anyone who wants to live a joyful life, you can carefully choose or tweak the description you are living so that you are continually empowered to be who you really are and to act accordingly. I can say with conviction and confidence, born of my own experiential knowledge, that a human being who acts in that awareness performs actions that have a unique power that is absent in a person who believes himself or herself to be a transient in a permanent world.

Sometimes metaphors can be quite literal

Having learned that the story I tell about myself is the most important factor in determining the quality of my experience, I have noticed that there are times when I am offered a look at striking connections between our language and our experience. What follows is a story that explains what I mean.

Several decades ago, I devoted a number of years to performing and travelling as a musician. My musical career allowed me the opportunity to make music with a number of talented drummers. While on a road gig, one particularly dear fellow developed a huge and extremely painful boil on one of his buttocks. As it would have been for any of us who sit down while making our music, this was a real challenge for him.

As this episode reached its peak, he and I had a conversation about what he was feeling. We considered the possibility that the boil somehow represented some thought or feeling he was not aware of but that was dominating his experience. In a moment of clarity he said, "I guess I have been considering myself to be a pain in the ass." Within minutes he looked at me with his face full of relief and told me that the boil had burst.

This was a great lesson for both of us. Seen from the perspective of the seer's explanation, not only were we given a glimpse of the connection between the story we tell and our resulting experience, but we also were shown that the Universe can have a rather outrageous sense of humor. To appreciate that, you have to be in the right frame of mind. You have to somehow transcend our habitual tendency to consider every experience as either a blessing or a curse and learn to see your life as a (mostly) gentle lesson in what it is to be a human being.

CHAPTER 15

WHAT HAPPENS WHEN WE CHANGE OUR STORY?

Testing the seer's explanation

When I was in school, we were taught the scientific method, which could be considered the crowning achievement of rational thought. It says that if you want to understand some aspect of the world, you develop a theory of that aspect and then examine the theory to find testable predictions. To the degree that the predictions confirm the theory, you feel entitled to increase your confidence that the theory is true or accurate. To the degree that the predictions are not borne out, however, you then have to modify the theory to account for these observations and try again.

I suggest that anyone who wants to test the theory that is the subject of this book—that what passes for the world is actually a description of the world—has only one domain in which to do the experiments, and that is one's own life experience. Actually, I'm suggesting that we've all been doing that experiment all along, for our entire lives. We have accepted an explanation for the appearance of the world and our place in it, and, sure enough, every experiment we've ever performed in our daily lives has confirmed that view. The result of that lifelong experiment, if one is paying attention and realizes that one is in fact conducting an experiment, is that the Universe is reflexive. It reflects back to you your understanding, your story about what you see. I'm only suggesting that we become deliberate about the experiment.

So, here's the experiment, the deliberate and conscious test of the idea that the world we experience is actually a story we learned to think of as the world: *tell a different story and see if the world begins to conform to that new view.* First, however, a caveat: if you decide to do that experiment honestly, I suspect you'll find right away that it's not as easy as it sounds. To me it's like considering a physical activity that you've been participating in for a long time. You might have developed bad habits that limit your success, such as a bad golf swing or an inefficient running gait. Changing those habits requires intense concentration, commitment, and often some coaching, and usually those habits take some time to overcome.

Habits of thought and belief behave the same way. It is one thing to work with a coach and modify some aspect of physical action, such as a golf swing, so that the desired result is gradually produced. It is quite another to change your view of the world so that you actually see that you are looking at a learned and consistently practiced description when you open your eyes in the morning. You have to change that story little by little. However, what I've discovered is that the Universe will help you out if you're actually *doing* the experiment, which is different from *thinking about* the experiment.

Of course, any such change of habit requires that we start someplace. With that in mind, is there a person in your life who is 'hard to love,' someone who really would have to change in some way before you can love or accept him or her? Does this person have some redeeming qualities? You always have the choice of where to focus your attention. So, you might try paying attention to those positive attributes whenever you can, and simply ignore the ones you don't like. Then, see if that person gradually shows up differently in your experience, more in accord with what you consider their positive qualities.

Doing this experiment honestly means you have to put aside what you already know about this person and put aside what you already know about people in general, which is that they are the way they are, and that's the end of it. In the process, you may even discover that the way people show up for you is a function of your expectations of them.

To generalize the lesson that is available in this experiment, what if *your emotional set-point* turns out to have something to do with how people show up for you in that moment, or even with *who* shows up? What if your experience of others is a function of the position of your assemblage point, which in turn is a function of the story you tell yourself? You may actually have the experience of watching someone else begin to be a different person in your eyes simply as a result of your willingness to look at people not as objects with fixed characteristics but as aspects of a reflexive Universe, one that reflects back to us our idea of the world. In that moment you can begin to sense your own power.

Stalking a new story

Juan Matus spent a considerable amount of time with Carlos Castaneda introducing him to the idea of 'stalking' as a technique to change one's idea of the world. To do that, he took Carlos out into the desert and taught him how to hunt. He pointed out that to hunt effectively you have to observe the prey carefully. He showed Carlos how to anticipate the animal's movements and regulate his own so that his presence and actions wouldn't alarm the animal. That task required great concentration, which had the added benefit of helping Carlos turn down the volume of his internal dialog.

The point of that exercise in stalking, however, was not to teach Carlos how to feed himself in the desert. It was to introduce the idea of stalking as a methodology that can be applied to oneself—watching for clues, and patterns, and evidence.

In this story, Matus was urging Castaneda to view the world as a mysterious, incomprehensible place where magical things can show up, things that we ordinarily don't notice because we already 'know' what the world is and how it operates. That's the idea of magic and mystery we need in order to honestly do the experiment I'm describing. So the question becomes, can we allow the world to be magical and mysterious?

Also, what does it mean to say that the Universe will help you out if you actually do the experiment? I'm suggesting that if you approach your daily life as an experiment to see if there are previously unnoticed indications that you have more power than you believed you have, you will find evidence that you do have that additional power. For example, suppose you are accustomed to the occasional 'coincidence' of someone reaching out to you just after you think about them. Suppose you begin to think of all those you care about as being connected by invisible threads that seem to defy your apparent physical separation. You might then interpret a significant increase in those 'coincidences' as a validation of your new thinking. Some folks say we're all connected by these threads!

So, to 'stalk' yourself is to make up your mind to trust yourself and the Universe. It is to watch for indications that the Universe hears you and will respond to what you want, but only to the degree that you allow yourself to let go of the culturally mandated obligation to *make* things happen by cleverness or contrivance or by sheer force of will. The ultimate experiment in the reflexive Universe is to consider yourself the source of the entirety of your own experience. Gradually drop all the blame and victimhood and the feeling of the need to compete with others. Gradually release the self-importance, the petty lying and bending of the truth. These are all things we do to get an advantage and skew the odds toward ourselves. A real Being in command of the totality of one's Self[8] would have no need of those contrivances. Let the Universe show you who you really are: complete, whole, and enough.

Stalking authenticity

One way I've discovered to approach the experience of the seer's explanation is to search for my own authenticity. As an example, one of my lifelong habits has been to respond to others' tales of difficulty and hardship with expressions of sympathy and commiseration. The problem with those expressions, on my part, is that even though they may produce some temporary measure of good feeling in myself or the other person, I know they are not genuine. I know myself well enough to understand that I don't really feel that way. As a result, I don't feel good when I try to 'be there' in that way for someone else in his or her time of difficulty.

Here's a story I tell myself about that. Imagine that you are lying out on some soft grass on a warm summer's night. You hear cries for help. After a bit of groping in the dark, you realize that the cries are coming from someone who is stuck at the bottom of a large pit with smooth sides that prohibit climbing out.

Being a wise person, you offer the 'victim' several choices. You say, "Well, I could sit here and tell you how badly I feel that you're stuck down in there. Or I could jump in there with

---

[8] Once again, I use the capitalized word Self to refer to the Self we really are, the 'inventor' Self. Due to the way we humans hear and interpret words, this makes it sound as if the Self is an object. This, however, is an illusion. This is an example of why it is so hard to speak of the domain of Being with words derived for use in the domain of Having.

you. But then there would be two of us who couldn't climb out." To me, those two suggestions represent sympathy and empathy, respectively.

However, consider the suggestion, "I assure you that there's a rope in there, the other end of which is tied to a sturdy tree. I'll coach you in finding it and in using it to climb out of the pit." This is something else entirely; it represents offering another person your accumulated wisdom, wisdom you've gained by being in the 'pit' yourself and learning how to climb out.

Before I encountered the seer's explanation, I thought there was something wrong with me that would explain why I wasn't any good at commiseration. However, I believe I have always known, at a deep level, that if I encounter difficulty, it's of my own making. I know now that I can always trace my problems to an inadequate or incomplete understanding of who I am and what is required for me to feel good about myself. In that sense, I know that my problems are a function of the story I tell about myself. And I have to conclude that's true of everyone else as well, no matter how daunting the challenges they may face. We have each created our own problems with the thoughts we have about ourselves and about the situations we find ourselves in. It takes effort to remember that the world we experience is a reflection of our thoughts and beliefs.

The racket

Each of us has a self-image to which we cling mightily. My self-image is that I am a kind and gentle person, warm and caring and considerate of all the people I encounter in my daily life. I like that self-image, and I'm happy to project it to everyone, old friends and new. The only problem is that it's a contrivance. It's part of who I learned to be to ensure that people would like me and include me so that I wouldn't be alone. I think that, by far, the most difficult thing any human being could possibly do is to allow that self-image to crumble so that the real Being can emerge. It's a terrifying prospect, giving up the mask that one has worn for so long and that we have fervently believed to be who we are. Who might we turn out to be?

Werner Erhard called this mask—this contrivance we adopted as children in an attempt to avoid feeling dominated and insecure—a 'racket.' Erhard defined a racket as a dishonest scheme involving activities that are in essence fraudulent. That definition, when applied to our masks, our public personas, makes them sound pretty awful, though quite accurately described. And to confront this mask, our own lack of authenticity, is enormously difficult for a human being. But it's also the doorway we have to pass through to discover who we really are.

Erhard went on to point out that every racket has both a payoff and a cost. The payoff of a racket is what one gets out of it. What I've gotten out of my racket is the feeling that I'm not alone, that people like me, and that I'm a good person. For me, the payoff of my racket has been consistently rewarding. I have always had friends who welcome me with open arms.

So, if this mask I've worn for so long is a racket, why in the world would I want to give it up? To be honest, I don't particularly *want* to give it up. It's just that I feel increasingly uncomfortable when I see my personality as a contrivance or as an act, which I seem to notice more and more. My 'sympathy racket,' which casts people as victims of circumstances, applies to me as well, and so it costs me my own authenticity and the power to determine my own quality of life. I simply can no longer forget hearing Werner Erhard say that the cost of one's racket is "only" love, health, happiness, and full self-expression.

CHAPTER 16

A QUESTION OF IDENTITY

The conventional view of 'I' and 'Me'

When we enter the world as babies, our parents begin to talk to us, usually from day one. In doing so, they are accomplishing two things, one of which is obvious and the other somewhat less so. What is obvious is that they are teaching us our native language. What is less obvious is that they are teaching us an understanding of the world which will in time allow us to function as separate, independent beings.

The words 'I' and 'Me' are first-person references to this separate being we believe ourselves to be, as distinct from the other beings we encounter. Those other beings become the second-person reference 'You,' and the third-person references 'They' and 'Them.' In this chapter, we will explore this idea of the first-person 'I' and 'Me', and we will examine the implications of this conventional dividing up of the world between what is 'Me' and what is not 'Me.'

First, we need to do some groundwork so that this exploration makes sense. Let's see if we can use a metaphor to visualize this different way of looking at the world, that when we think we're looking at the world, we're actually looking at a description of the world.

The world as a work of art

I engaged in the study of physics as an early expression of my desire to understand how the world, and thus life, works. These many decades later, it appears to me as if that whole discipline in an academic context is an effort to find the 'right' description of the physical world, an objective description that would eventually be refined or corroborated by anyone who seeks to understand it.

We humans always think that our description of the world is a picture of something that's 'out there,' some external reality. But what if our description is *all there is*, a self-reflecting story that we've inherited and then expanded and embellished and that we'll pass on to the next generation of 'describers'? What if we were to discover that our descriptions amount to nothing more than an 'artful' story we've been telling ourselves all these generations?

PAINTING OUR STORY ON THE WORLD

Then we could think of the physical world as a canvas upon which we paint our story, using description as our paint! Wouldn't that free us from having the 'right' description? Maybe then we could seek explanations that empower and enable us, or that bring us more joy, rather than the ones that are 'true.'

From the perspective of the seer's explanation, what we think of as the physical universe is not an 'is,' but is actually a universally accepted *description* of something Juan Matus called 'utterly mysterious and unfathomable.' This distinction makes a difference. You have little power over an 'is,' an actual physical *thing*, especially a thing as big as the world you experience. However, you do have power over a description; you can describe that *thing* in a different way, by 'painting' a different story about it.

Exploring 'Me' and 'not-Me'

As I've said before, when we open our eyes and look at the world as an 'is,' we see ourselves and each other as physical objects, bodies, placed in a context called the world. In terms of my inherited belief system, my physical identity ends at a boundary called my skin. If I identify myself with my body, I then conclude that who I am ends there as well.

Is that a real distinction, between myself on the one hand and everything and everybody else I see on the other? We take that distinction for granted, but does it hold up under scrutiny? Probably the strongest argument for it, in an experiential sense, is that most of us have physical sensations and motor control as a result of stimulation of nerve endings throughout the volume of space occupied by our bodies. Most of us would also say that we have neither sensations nor motor control beyond those boundaries.

However, adopting the seer's explanation caused me to abandon the idea of space as the ultimate context or container of our lives and replace it with awareness. In my awareness, in my *experience*, there is only 'here' when considering location. No one has ever experienced 'there.' Every time you move your body to a location you previously considered to be 'there,' you then find yourself 'here.' Now, let me say that 'there' certainly exists as an idea, as a concept; but it does not exist within the domain of experience, of what is truly *real*. When you learn to view the world from the vantage point of the seer's explanation, the idea you previously thought of as 'out there' disappears as a real place or direction.

The conventional understanding I received from our shared culture requires that I think of myself as an object among objects, with all that implies. We will continue to inquire further into the implications of considering ourselves objects among objects. For now, I am just suggesting the possibility that the distinction we all make between 'me' and 'not me' on the physical level is an artificial one. If all that I see, hear, touch, taste, and smell is part of a story I have learned to tell, *it's all me*! The idea that there is something 'out there,' something that is not me, would in that context turn out to be nothing more than a superstition.

Support from quantum physics

Years after I read Castaneda, I came to realize that my study of physics would prove useful in exploring what it means to say that separating the world into 'me' and 'not-me' is an artificial distinction. Quantum physics includes an idea referred to as non-locality. One of the intuitive ideas that we abstract from our common sense understanding of reality is that the separation among physical objects in space is real and independent of us as observers. However, in quantum experiments, physicists have seen that a pair of small objects, once interacting, acquire an identity as a pair. Then, flying off to great distances between them, *they continue to act as if they are one object with one set of properties.* This phenomenon, called entanglement, appears to violate our intuitive understanding of locality, the idea that each object appears to have a separate location in space.

However, non-locality appears to complement the realization I noted previously, that a human being can only experience 'here.' Again, 'there' is a concept and can never be experienced. So, seeing with our eyes that some object, or someone else, is 'over there' is something that can never be experienced *but only conceptualized as a three-dimensional picture formed by our brains from nothing but electrical impulses.* Everything we experience, up to and including our perception of the entire physical universe, is actually 'here.'

I'm suggesting that the distinction between 'me' and 'not me' on the physical level may be a superstition. I'm not claiming that suggestion is right or true. Asking if it is true amounts to asking if the seer's explanation is true, and I'm saying that's the wrong question. The better question is, does the choice to look at life from the seer's explanation give me more power to live a joyful life as a free being than the explanation that I am an object among objects?

What are the implications of the idea that everything within your field of view, at all times, is your own creation? The belief that consciousness resides in a particular object in space called a body is one of the foundational beliefs that underlie our world view. However, the awareness that everything in my field of view, including my body, makes up a description that I learned to perceive is incompatible with that belief and thus to the world view upon which it rests. That description amounts to my metaphorical painting on the canvas.

If that is the case, what do the words 'I' and 'Me' actually refer to? I'm suggesting that they don't refer to a body with conscious awareness, or to an object of any kind, as our commonsense idea would have it. Rather, they apply to the Self as a painter who applies the paint to the canvas of the world, to the Self as a poet who paints a picture with his or her words. Yes, that's a very abstract understanding of a human being, and many people may well not be comfortable with it. And yet, the ideas presented in this chapter leave me with no choice but to pursue insight and understanding of our Selves as abstract beings without boundaries.

CHAPTER 17

LIVING THE SEER'S EXPLANATION

The seer's explanation – a summary

The first of my three propositions is that the world we believe we are interacting with is actually a *description* of the world rather than the world itself.

The elements which make up this description are a collection of symbols we use to interpret, manage, and communicate about the sensory input to which we are constantly exposed. In the context of the standard, culturally derived idea of the world, those symbols refer to all the objects with which we're familiar, including our own bodies. In addition, they refer to all the types of events we witness in which these objects can interact with one another.

By way of example, I cited earlier a particular collection of visual and tactile vibrational impressions that I interpret as a kitchen counter. When I say I'm looking at that kitchen counter, what I'm doing is distinguishing that specific collection of impressions and sensations from the background. The background, in turn, is composed of the remainder of the impressions and sensations my brain receives. The counter is one of the elements of the description of my kitchen. Often, I forget that what I'm looking at is a description and not something 'out there' that's independent of my looking at it. But I'm getting better at it!

The second proposition I have argued is that this description on which we're focused serves as a recognizable, stable, and coherent platform on which to live our lives.

On this platform, provided for us by the Universe, we can explore the range of options of action that we can think of and then select for ourselves a path among those options, a path through life. We call this description on which we're focused, 'our world.'

To illustrate this second proposition, consider that I need a description of the objects within my field of view before I can contemplate what I can do with them. So, I have isolated within my visual field a kitchen counter and a laptop, as well as the all-important coffee cup. Now I can consider locating the laptop on the counter so that it stays in one place and I can interact with it. Furthermore, I know that by performing a particular sequence of actions using my body and the laptop, I can generate and observe a pattern of dots appearing on the screen. I can then interpret this pattern as a representation of the ideas and thoughts I have. This illustration serves as an example of what I would call 'operating my knowledge of the world.'

Now I have an explanation for the presence of all the objects within my field of view and for my presence among them. I have assembled all these objects in relation to my body so that I can use the laptop to write this book, and I can use the coffee cup and its contents to sharpen my focus.

I have, of course, left out myriad details in setting down this explanation. That leaving-out process is an example of the way I filter out all the symbols—and all my thoughts about those symbols—that are not necessary to get these ideas onto the screen. Examples of what got filtered out include all the thoughts that were not relevant and all the other objects that play no part in getting my thoughts onto the screen.

The third of my propositions goes as follows: the description I use to make sense of the world is the one I learned from the people with whom I interacted when I was young. As the use of this description became second nature to me, I mistook it for something largely external to me. It came to represent something over which I had no control.

As I sit here in my chair, it seems as if there is a world around me, 'out there.' If I then choose to get out of my chair and do something, it seems as if I will then be living out into the world. However, if the world out there is actually a description and not the world itself, I will be getting up and living out into my description of the world.

Ultimately, *by recognizing that I have mistaken the description of the world for the world itself, I now have a new explanation to live from, one in which I am the context in which my world exists and not the other way around.* I call this new explanation the seer's explanation.

Why it matters which explanation we choose

On this path of discovery, I have learned that it really matters which explanation I choose to live from. Normally, we think of the ability to determine the quality of our lives as residing 'out there' in the world, principally in the actions of other people. But what if I have the power to determine my own experience?

In that case, I find myself with a range of choices that differ considerably from those I would have if I gave away my power to others.

The difference between those two possibilities is about as great as any two possibilities could be. You can stick with an explanation of the world you already know, and then seek to change through action the quality of your life one choice at a time. However, what you're really doing is rearranging the existing set of options into some other configuration.

Or you can adopt a different explanation, such as the seer's explanation, and decide to live it. In this case, an entirely new set of choices appears. In my direct experience, the difference between those approaches is between going through the motions, on the one hand, and living as if life is a daring adventure (to paraphrase a famous quote from Helen Keller) on the other. In this light, choosing an explanation to live from requires shifting the basis on which you make the choice. Our culture has trained us to make that choice based on the supposed truth of a culturally derived explanation. In contrast, I recommend choosing an explanation based on its ability to reconnect you with your natural power, the unlimited creativity of the Self as an artist painting on the canvas of life.

Let's examine a number of aspects of life from the point of view of the seer's explanation. I want to emphasize over and over that I believe it's useless to evaluate this new explanation in the context of deciding whether or not it's true. I have, however, found during the course of my life that living as if it were true has brought me a sense of peace and personal power which I had not found in living from the 'normal,' culturally derived explanation.

Implications of losing the human form

Earlier I suggested that the distinction between 'me' and 'not-me' on the physical level may be a superstition. Juan Matus referred to that distinction as 'losing the human form.'

What are the implications of abandoning the human form? This implies releasing the belief that the dividing line between you and not-you is your skin. I suggest that if you honestly examine the possibility of doing that, one of the first things that happens is that you begin to lose the feeling that you're living in a dangerous world. I use the phrase 'begin to lose the feeling' to indicate that this shift doesn't happen all at once; it seems that patience and steadfastness are required to gain this result.

The idea of danger sits on top of the belief that you are your body, and your body is an object among objects. If there are objects outside of you that can act upon you against your will, then those objects can adversely affect you. This is the case whether those objects are active objects like other people, or passive objects such as the weather, illnesses, or the economy.

Also, notice that the belief that you are an object among objects is required by, and actually leads to, the feeling of being a victim. You can't be a victim when you are painting the entirety of the world you experience. You observe the behavior of other objects out there as they appear to affect you. If you couple that observation with the obvious fact that you can't control those objects, you will eventually be left with the feeling of being a victim of others or of circumstances. This in turn leaves you feeling powerless. Embracing all that you see as your own creation causes that entire victimhood racket to crumble.

Now, there's good news and bad news about that. The bad news is that, for most of us, the feeling of being a victim is a key component of the strategies we have developed for dealing with other people, particularly people in perceived positions of power relative to us. In other words, the feeling of being a victim is an essential part of almost everybody's racket. What's the payoff of that racket? The payoff is that we have someone or something to blame when we don't get what we want. It's much easier to settle for that thought than to recognize that we have some belief that is keeping us from feeling worthy of what we wanted. The cost of that victim racket is the loss of our own power. Changing beliefs that have been experientially validated for a lifetime is extremely hard work; feeling like a victim is much easier.

The challenge of changing our thoughts

Once you realize that you are creating all that you see, it becomes clear that there are no objects outside of you. There are only possibilities, and possibilities only become actualized in your experience when you focus your undivided attention on them. Fortunately for you, and for all of us, simply having a thought doesn't make it actualize in your experience. For something to actualize, a creative being has to focus attention on it, feed it, and give it a life of its own. I say 'fortunately,' because my mind often seems full of thoughts that I would never want to find their way into my experience. Because thoughts don't actualize until they have been fed and nurtured, there is a lag between the thought and the manifestation that allows one to change the subject or the tone of the thought.

That time lag, however, turns out to be a challenge for someone stalking his or her own power. If you experience an unpleasant event in your life, and it occurs to you that there is a better way of looking at that event—a way for you to sense your power—you may well not experience a sudden transformation that changes everything and gives you a powerful reinforcement of your re-interpretation. You usually have to practice the new thinking, just as if you were seeking to change a bad habit into a good one. Because you have practiced the self-limiting interpretation for such a long time, it takes more time for the new habit of thought to become sufficiently dominant in order to change the way that topic manifests in your life. One can get discouraged. The antidote to that difficulty is persistence. I can say from my own experience that eventually the desire for change will be strong enough that persistence becomes progressively easier.

There are also many techniques available for making this process a bit easier. I think that the most powerful class of such techniques is those that help quiet the internal dialog. It is difficult to notice that a particular event triggers a negative or self-limiting thought process if the overall volume of thought is too high. I have noticed that when I fail to consistently practice that calming of the mind, I spend large portions of my day failing to notice the distinction between myself and the din of what I've often called 'the voice in my head.' By far the most powerful tool I have at my disposal is the meditation I was taught back in 1973; as it happens, I've been practicing that technique for almost fifty years.

If meditation is not for you, you might try other methods for quieting the mind. Juan Matus introduced Carlos Castaneda to one such technique, which he called 'the right way of walking.' I have found that technique useful as well, so I'll include it here. 'The right way of walking' amounts to walking while paying attention to everything in your field of view, including your peripheral vision. The effort to continuously perform that task leaves little energy for feeding the mind's excessive motion through its trains of thought.

What is important here is intent. If your intention is to quiet your mind, and if you stay present to that effort, almost any activity will do.

CHAPTER 18

THE SEER'S EXPLANATION AS LEVERAGE

"Give me a lever... and I shall move the world" -- Archimedes

As European expansion in the New World brought agriculture to heavily forested land, settlers confronted natural obstacles, objects such as tree stumps and boulders which they needed to remove. Naturally, the effort to accomplish this clearing was often beyond the abilities of even the strongest.

People needed a way to apply more force to these tasks, and the principle of leverage underlaid their more successful efforts, whether it involved tools or animals.

The earliest evidence of people using a lever mechanism was about 7,000 years ago, but Archimedes, a Greek scientist from the 3rd century BCE, understood the principle more thoroughly than anyone before him. He said, "Give me a lever long enough and a fulcrum on which to place it, and I shall move the world."

ARCHIMEDES AND HIS LEVER

The principle of leverage is well understood in manipulating the physical world, but it can be applied to improving our experience of living as well. In order to appreciate this possibility, we'll need to make some distinctions about where and how such leverage might be used in our relationship to the world around us. First, we'll need to understand the power of the present moment, as distinct from that of our memories of the past and our anticipation of the future.

Experience versus thoughts about experience

Earlier, I made the statement that our entire linguistic inventory arose to deal with the domains of Doing and Having, or events and objects. By extension, that's true of the human mind as well. What the mind is good at is rationality: sifting and sorting the records of past experience and the meaning the mind ascribes to those experiences. For the vast majority of human beings, rationality is what our culture has taught us is most important in finding solutions to problems.

In terms of the story our culture tells us about who we are, we tend to hold rationality in high regard; you can see that regard in the word 'irrational,' which usually carries a derogatory meaning. Juan Matus, however, called rationality, or reason, 'puny.' He claimed that rationality is only effective within the bounds of its natural domain, sorting through the information we have collectively managed to gather. "It craps out," as he put it, when faced with questions that lie outside of that domain. Any inquiry into what else is possible for human beings—beyond that which we already know about—falls into that category.

Earlier, I defined what I call knowing-without-language. This knowing beyond the accumulation of facts is an experiential knowing that becomes available to us as we learn to quiet the internal dialog. I see this type of knowing as a connection with the source of all knowledge. It is sometimes called intuition, a word that is given less weight than rationality by the broader culture which does not recognize the existence of consciousness not contained within a body.

Everything that has ever been imagined or that has ever existed is held by and within the Universe, the universal consciousness of which each of us is an individual expression. Those two different kinds of knowing, 'information-gathering' and 'knowledge-without-language' are generally not seen as distinct from one another. Most humans have lost the knowledge of our innate connection to universal knowledge, to the wisdom of All-that-Is. As a result, we are left with knowledge as information-gathering and sorting, which is truly 'puny' by comparison.

When we spend some time practicing just being, just being aware without the internal dialog, thoughts do arise spontaneously. However, these thoughts are of a different nature than rational ones; they have a different quality. Our real Selves also have thoughts, revealed as we practice quieting the voice in our heads. The thoughts of our inner beings are exciting and life-giving because they represent new possibilities, and new possibilities come from who and what we really are. They are positive, and they always feel good.

Experience lives in the domain of knowledge-without-language, the domain of Being, which is distinct from thought. For the most part, we're not even aware of our experience, because it so quickly becomes memory. To really experience, to savor experience, you actually have to postpone the turning of the experience into thought, into a memory. The present moment of experience is also the only place we can apply the leverage required to effectively improve the quality of life.

Using a lever instead of brute force

Along this path of discovery, I have found that action is much more powerful when leveraged by first changing my feelings. Until I began to understand the seer's explanation, I thought that by sharpening my rational decision-making I could make better decisions and that doing so was the most efficient way to improve how I felt. What I've noticed, however, is that when I act in the world from rationality, from trying to figure things out and make things happen, action contains the quality of effort. And in a world where every action provokes an equal and opposite reaction, it takes a great deal of effort to change anything.

Just as a lever greatly increases your effectiveness in moving a heavy object, emotionally leveraged action is much more powerful than un-leveraged action. The leverage comes from changing your feelings to those that are a closer match to those felt by your inner Being, your real Self. It follows then that the best use of effort is to quiet the internal dialog, listen to your heart, and find out how you really feel. The lesson is, don't expend your effort lifting your metaphorical rocks; expend it getting a lever in place instead.

The effort to remember to do this, to practice meditation, to practice Juan Matus's right way of walking, to spend time in nature, or employing any other technique you find useful, pays off in ways unimaginable to the rational mind. Interestingly, leveraged action, stemming as it does simply from wanting to find a way to feel better, tends to threaten the Ego, the invented self. It can feel like an attempt to put it out of business. The Ego resists that attempt mightily, which may account in part for the need to practice these techniques with great consistency.

An example of applying emotional leverage

My wife and I have a rental unit in our backyard. For a time, it was rented to a gentleman who, unbeknownst to us, experienced a powerful episode of PTSD, post-traumatic stress disorder. This episode resulted in physical damage to our rental, and it triggered strong feelings of anger in us. We wanted him 'out of there!'

We met with a legal advisor to clarify any options we might have in terminating his lease early, and we were told that those options were expensive and quite limited. In view of the time remaining on his lease, it might be more trouble to 'get rid of him' than it was worth.

This advice left us feeling that we had lost control of the situation, and that didn't feel good. At that point, we explored other possible 'stories,' other ways we could frame the situation that would feel better. We recognized that here was an opportunity to reach beneath the feelings of fear and betrayal and seek a place of true compassion for what our renter was going through. We were able to embrace that compassion, and this allowed us to feel much better about the situation.

By the time he fulfilled his lease and departed on the next chapter of his life, we had understood that the lesson, and our opportunity, was to surrender to what might be called the 'path of least resistance.' We had clearly expressed our preference for him to depart. However, allowing the situation to play out enabled us to find a relationship of compassion rather than one of conflict. It is clear to us that this unfolding involved far less resistance than any action we might have taken to pry him out of the unit. And it promoted an ending to that landlord/tenant relationship with civility and mutual respect. This was another great lesson in finding the best-feeling story we can and then permitting whatever consequences might ensue.

The idea of self-worth as leverage

As I write these words, the world is in the midst of a coronavirus pandemic. Global efforts to combat this pandemic, such as stay-at-home orders and business closures, have resulted in significant reductions in economic activity. It is said over and over today that the economies of many countries in the world are in real trouble, thus causing real suffering for millions of people. We, here in the United States, seem to be mired in arguments about the perils of doing too much to combat the downturn versus doing too little. Trying to fix the economy feels very much like heavy lifting by brute force.

There is enormous suffering and pain the world over associated with the economic situation in which we find ourselves today. I have no desire to minimize the devastation of the real experience of finding oneself without shelter or adequate food. However, let us consider whether there is leverage available to make life easier and where that leverage might be applied.

Let's start by considering, again, the word 'economy.' That word, of course, points to an abstraction. No one has ever seen an economy the way we see common objects. The word 'economy' labels an abstraction with which we can grasp the totality of a system in which goods and services are exchanged.

We are all members of cultures that define the terms of this exchange with quantities like 'value' and 'worth.' We use those quantities to identify and measure economic flow, which can be thought of as the circulatory system of the world body. We don't have to think about this abstraction called the economy. In fact, we don't. We use it because we all agree on its meaning, but most of us never look deeply and carefully into that meaning. We humans believe strongly in measurement, but when we measure economic quantities, we assume we are measuring some 'is,' some aspect of a system that lies outside of ourselves.

The seer's explanation, however, reminds us that *there is nothing outside of ourselves*. When we think we are looking at some real, independent phenomenon, we are actually looking at our own interpretation or description of that phenomenon. As such, we are projecting the ideas of value and worth, largely as they apply to ourselves, 'outwards' onto a description of the world that we've mistaken for the world itself.

Very few of us have ever looked objectively at our own ideas of self-value and self-worth. In my case, I assumed since childhood that the opinions of those 'others' are more objective and reliable than how I really feel about myself. Over many decades, and with much effort, I have come to see that other people's opinions of me are mostly about themselves and are projections of their own sense of self-worthiness. They're not really about me at all.

During the current period of economic stress, most of us have agreed that the pandemic, and the social distancing that appears to be required to combat it, are responsible for the stress the vast majority of us are feeling. This conclusion clearly places the cause of our negative feelings on conditions outside of ourselves, on the circumstances in which we find ourselves. These conditions and circumstances, of course, are almost completely out of our control. When we blame the economy for our stress, we lose our power to make a difference in our experience.

The seer's explanation, on the other hand, reminds us to regard the circumstances we face as a reflection of our (mostly suppressed) feelings about ourselves. So, when we face limited access to the goods and services we say we want, those limitations validate our limited idea of ourselves. And, in the process, they serve to perpetuate our racket. They serve to justify decisions we have made about ourselves that have profound consequences in our physical experience. Our beliefs about ourselves cause our experiences, and our experiences then reinforce our beliefs, and so on in the vicious circle I described earlier.

'The' economy as individual self-image

In view of all the above, I believe that what we're left with is that the blockage of economic flow lives in an individual human being's self-image, and in the resulting description and interpretation of the world he or she perceives. As I noted previously, that's why there are people who thrive in every bad economy, and there are people who suffer in every good one.

There is no domestic or global economy as an 'is'; the seer's explanation says that the existence of a single economy 'out there' is in fact a superstition. Furthermore, for a real Self, for who we really are, *there is no restriction of any kind.* Restriction, in the sense we've been using the word, can only arise in the mind of an individual who has forgotten who he or she really is. When we look at an economy in a downturn, we are actually looking at the manifestation of a collective amnesia. We have all forgotten who and what we really are.

That we are collective amnesiacs is the bad news. The good news is that for you to move from the experience of depravation to the experience of plenty, nobody else needs to change a thing. You change your idea of who you are, and the Universe will, over time, effortlessly and seamlessly accommodate you. You change your understanding of scarcity and abundance from objective facts to an emotional choice, and then you watch for clues that the world gradually conforms to your new story.

As you do that, other people will no doubt eventually notice the difference in you, and they will have whatever opinions they'll have about that. You may find some people drifting out of your experience and others drifting in. I can say it is an amazingly good feeling when you sense your power to live your dreams, especially if they appear to require money to manifest themselves. What before appeared to require a great deal of effort to overcome, such as 'not having as much money as you need,' now appears as a wonderful adventure in which you never know where the next delightful surprise will show up. You have opened yourself to previously unseen possibilities.

There is one more fortuitous aspect to looking at the shift from scarcity to abundance from the seer's perspective. You don't have to do it all at once. Earlier, we talked about the idea of stalking oneself. We considered the possibility of viewing the world as a 'mysterious, unfathomable' place where magical things can show up, things that we ordinarily don't notice because we already 'know' what the world is and how it operates. Most of us have no real experience of magical occurrence. I can say, however, that if you make the effort to even be willing to change your idea of yourself and the world, the Universe will meet you more than halfway. You don't need to 'stop the world,' as I did that one day with my gas tank. Just look for clues and expect to find them. It's well worth the effort.

CHAPTER 19

THE TRANSFORMATIVE POWER OF THE SEER'S EXPLANATION

About financial independence

With this discussion of abundance (or lack thereof) firmly in mind, let's talk about personal financial independence. The phrase conjures up images of Having: having lots of money, income, investments, financial instruments, and the like. And, of course, that brings up questions about how much is enough, what about inflation and the ups and downs of markets, etc.

It seems to me that if we look from the conventional explanation of who we are and what the world is, there's a lot to consider before one can declare oneself financially independent. We live in a world which exhibits a great deal of uncertainty. Businesses come and go. Some promises get kept and others don't. Expectations are met, or not. In a world in which there's only enough 'stuff' to go around, we are forced to compete with one another, and the actions of others can impact what we are able to gather up and how much of that we are able to hang onto.

That's the conventional interpretation of reality: the 'stuff' of life is real, and there's only so much of it, and so we have to strive to gain more, and to protect what we have. The seer's explanation, on the other hand, turns that interpretation of reality upside down. Yes, the stuff of life is real, but it's not as real as we are! So, there must be another way to look at the idea of financial independence, one in which things aren't so uncertain.

For me, the way to begin is to look first at what I really want. Do I want lots of money, large numbers on a screen or pieces of paper issued by a bank or similar institution? Or do I really want the life experience that I believe those large numbers will bring me? When I get right down to it, what I really want is to *feel* independent, free to make the choices I wish to make, unfettered by the feelings associated with statements such as 'I can't afford that.'

Here's where the seer's explanation comes in handy. It says that *the world shows up in accordance with the story I tell about my life*. Can I really just start telling a different story, one in which many of my oft-declared financial limitations don't appear? Yes. Certainly, it requires practice to do that. Plus, I don't necessarily have the answers about what it looks like to get from scarcity to abundance. But Universal intelligence does, and I am an expression of that intelligence. Actually, it already knows how to get me from here to there. So, what's in the way? What's in the way is all my beliefs to the contrary.

What if I could really accept that whenever I fully commit myself to follow a given path, the resources required to fulfill that path will appear? That would be true financial independence. It wouldn't require having anything but what I need at the moment. It wouldn't require large numbers of people (markets) to behave in any particular manner. And it doesn't require any certainty besides the certainty with which I know who I really am (my Self).

There's one more thought I'd like to offer on this topic of telling a different story about finances. I just talked about fully committing myself to a particular path. If the resources required to fulfill that path don't seem to be appearing, I could lose faith in this 'new-story' process. However, I could instead question the degree to which I'm committed to it. When the resources don't appear right away, I choose to examine my thoughts for any beliefs that contradict my sense that I deserve to follow the 'path with heart.' Examples of these contradictory beliefs could be 'I'm not worthy,' 'Being wealthy is just luck,' or 'Money is evil.' They're always there!

The true nature of freedom

People whose rational minds were nurtured in this culture of ours, me included, have learned to view our society as dysfunctional and our world as in desperate need of repair. We see innumerable problems in both our society and our world, and many of us feel a strong need to exert effort in finding and implementing solutions. We see our range of approaches to these problems as living in the domain of action, and very much in the context of trying to convince others of the truth of our views.

We correctly sense that the power of action, especially for individuals, is limited. So, we identify with groups, often political parties, whose size *seems* to give us more leverage. We either see ourselves as members of the political majority that happens to be in power at present, or we identify ourselves as members of the current minority. In either case, we tend to feel righteous and defensive about our ideas, and antagonistic toward others who have a different perspective.

One of the central threads of this often heated discussion is a misunderstanding of the nature of freedom. We all agree that freedom is a positive aspect of life, and bondage is a negative. However, when we talk about public policy as it pertains to freedom, we tend to argue within the context of our belief that we are separate, competitive beings. What restrictions, if any, should be placed on the behavior of individuals or groups of individuals? When do such restrictions, when put in place in 'the public interest,' become undue impediments to the individual's right and freedom to choose?

Due to our self-identification as rational beings, and because the effectiveness of rationality is confined to its rather limited domain, we are forced to think of freedom as being something that is relative, under attack, or perhaps just missing. In other words, we believe in the scarcity of freedom. In terms of the current political debate, either our freedom appears to be threatened by some other person or group's idea of fairness or safety, or our freedom seems to have been taken away by an unfair distribution of wealth and power.

We cling to our belief in scarcity, which is an inevitable logical result of seeing ourselves as objects among objects. Within that belief, everything we value in life is seen to be in finite supply. This gives rise to life as a zero-sum game, in which if you get more of something we both value, I must get less. This idea applies to money, desirable objects, potential lovers or mates, good jobs, and so on. If I believe I have some power to exert (actually, force), and if I see another group of people as competing with me for what I value, I may well try to use that power to force them to live within certain boundaries that keep them away from me and my territory. And, of course, the reverse is also true. Obviously, that's been going on as long as we have been human beings; in fact, that sort of competition seems to be wired into most animal species, including ours.

However, the seer's explanation says that *the idea that we are objects among objects is a superstition.* It also says that *we process sensory stimuli according to the way we were taught to see the world.* If you try the seer's explanation on for size, you may see that there is nothing 'out there' that can affect our freedom. Who we really are, our true Self, is completely free, and the only way for our freedom to be curtailed is to *believe* that others have power over us. To quote Esther Hicks, "You are so free you can choose bondage."

The seer's explanation says that *what each of us sees as the world is actually our own description of the world.* The Universe, with its infinite range of possibilities, blends everyone's description together into a coherent whole. And this whole is so seamless, we don't even notice that we've mistaken the description of the world for the world itself. With that explanation in mind, we can see that no other person can assert themselves into our experience. My experience is a function of the interpretation of the sensory input I receive—and the world I create as a result—and of that interpretation alone. Going back to a previous example, if I interpret the world as a dangerous place, it's entirely possible, even probable, that someone may show up whose intentions appear dangerous to me.

Once again, according to the seer's explanation, *the idea of danger rests upon believing that we are objects among objects.* If we come to see that interpretation as a superstition, danger evaporates as an interpretation as well. Without danger as a feature of our description of the world, people with 'dangerous' proclivities will either not manifest those proclivities in our experience, or they simply will not show up while we're around. If you can free yourself from the idea that there is one world we all are stuck with, you will see the bad stuff in the world for what it is: a manifestation of energy consistent with the expectations of the people who experience it.

People show up in my experience in accord with the way I see myself and my world. We are all capable of showing up in multiple vibrational modes. I know, for example, that I am capable of a wide range of moods and attitudes, as is everyone else. So, when someone enters my experience, they will tend to show up for me in a manner consistent with my general mood at the time. Seen in that light, I'm the one controlling what sort of people appear in my experience.

The media, the news, and the default explanation

There is, I think, a strong argument for weaning ourselves from a preoccupation with the news. Someone who watches or reads the news with any consistency may well come to feel that the world is terribly broken. They will probably also acquire a very cynical attitude about the motivations and inclinations of other people, especially people in positions of relative power. Some people may think of the news as simple information, and watching it as exercising the responsible person's obligation to stay informed. But the news isn't just information. In our culture it's always prepared within a particular explanation, within a particular view of the world, and it's delivered from a particular perspective. And finally, it isn't complete; it doesn't cover the full range of activities in which people are engaged.

One may have thought that the shift from the half-hour news shows we had in the 1960s to the so-called twenty-four-hour news cycle would have vastly expanded the scope of coverage. But the news actually represents a viewpoint, the 'Tonal of the times,' the predominant explanation within which the vast majority of people operate their knowledge of the world. The expansion of the availability of news has only enlarged the inventory of manifestations of that viewpoint, not the range of possibilities. The seer's explanation says *the dominant paradigm in the world today is what makes the world show up as it does for all of us who share that perspective.*

If you watch commercial television, you are subjected not only to the news and its clear orientation toward the problems of the world, but also to the commercials. Some of these are relatively innocuous, though they do expose viewers to endless reiterations of the dominant worldview. Some are even great fun, such as some of those shown during the Super Bowl. However, many of them pointedly serve to perpetuate feelings of negativity regarding the nature of the world. Witness the commercials for security services, insurance companies, and lawyers, in particular those with a specialty in injury or tort law. Commercials for weight-loss products tend to get viewers focused on their current physical shape and size, rather than their promised results. And the winner of the rub-your-nose-in-it sweepstakes may be ads for prescription medications, which serve to remind us of how many ways the body can go wrong.

One implication of the seer's explanation as it pertains to the dominant worldview is that the news—and the commercials—play a central role in the perpetuation of the world's problems we spoke of earlier in this chapter. According to the seer's explanation, *it is the continued focus of our attention that causes a particular configuration of energy, as expressed in a particular grouping or bundling of thoughts, to show up as real physical experience.*

Our culture has trained us to put a premium on 'telling it like it is.' We are told to stay informed, and in the effort to do so, we wind up subjecting ourselves to the way mass consciousness looks at everything. However, I invite you to consider the possibility that if you withdraw your attention from acting on the feeling that you *need* to stay informed about the world, and instead focus consistently on what brings you joy and good feelings, the world you experience will morph into one that is more to your liking.

However, I find myself fascinated by watching the news for signs that the evolution of human beings is well underway. I will put forth my belief in the reality of that process shortly. For now, I bring it up simply as another 'place' from which to view the news. At present, watching for these evolutionary signs is a bit like the inefficiency of panning for gold, but then, it's a good lesson in patience!

Anyway, if you do the work necessary to change your viewpoint towards one that feels better, the community you live in will either gradually turn into the one you desire, or you will find yourself with good, logical reasons to find another one that will. And when that happens, you will hear the clamor of the news, and the political posturing it records, as just so much of what Shakespeare's Macbeth called "sound and fury signifying nothing."

Illness and the body as an indicator

I think a fair warning is in order: This section may stir strong feelings of resistance. As counterintuitive as it may sound, we human beings seem to be overly attached to our illnesses, our bodily conditions, and our diagnoses. In terms of the way we relate our stories to one another in the normal course of events, these topics are very often the first to be brought up. It may be that this aspect of shared experience makes us feel not-alone at a deep level.

In one sense, these stories may feed our victim rackets; the sympathy our tales of woe engender seems to be very compelling. In another sense, they are the result of, and serve to mask, feelings we would prefer not to face. If you consider yourself or someone close to you to have an illness or unpleasant diagnosis, I urge you to pay attention to your feelings as you read the following paragraphs.

From the viewpoint of the normal, culturally derived idea of a human being, our bodies are essentially machines. They are part of the world, the world we all 'know' to be a mechanical reality that acts and evolves according to well-established rules. One can certainly argue that the human body is far more complex and finely tuned than any man-made machine. Yet, like all other machines in our experience, we assume that our bodies and the way they function are largely independent from our thoughts and attitudes about them.

Recall that the seer's explanation tells us: *everything in the world of our experience, everything we see, hear, and so on, is an interpretation of sensory input.* We assume that the interpretation, the picture of the world in our minds, is an accurate representation of what's actually 'out there.' I hope that, having read this far, you are at least willing to entertain the idea that there is no 'out there' except as part of the interpretation you are making. If so, you may also decide to contemplate the idea that the world of your interpretations is shaped and colored by your past experience and by the beliefs you hold. In that case, since your body is part of the interpretation you call the world, your view of your body is conditioned by those factors as well.

The relationship between stress and bodily ills is well known. As I write these words, I am reminded of a recent cancellation of a planned trip to visit our grandson, due to winter travel in the mountains. Contemplating that drive created resistance in me, and the stress showed up right away in my lower back. That part of my anatomy has proven to be a reliable indicator of my level of stress, and I have learned through experience to take that indication seriously. I have trained myself to treat the stress and not just the sore back.

I suggest to you that we cannot separate the reality of our bodies from our experience of them and specifically from our conditioned interpretation of anything and everything we think is wrong with them. We don't just have ailments; we also have all the meaning we have placed on those ailments: what we did wrong, all our bad habits with regard to our physical selves, and everything others told us about our bodies that we internalized and carry around inside us.

From that perspective, we can see that our bodies reflect back to us all the thoughts, beliefs, and attitudes we have about them. Among all the objects in my field of view, I most closely identify my body with my sense of self. As a result, I can view my body as an indicator of the well-being of my own self-image. Ok, how do you most effectively use the body as an indicator of the well-being of your self-image? The first thing you have to do is stop regarding physical 'issues' as proof that something is wrong.

The truth is, there is absolutely nothing wrong with my body. Referring once again to my gas-tank experience, it turned out that there was nothing wrong with my gas gauge. It actually was telling me what was going on, as improbable as I then considered that reality. In fact, from the perspective of the seer's explanation, *everything is working perfectly.* As I gain more experience with this new explanation, I find that when my body doesn't feel good, I remember more quickly that

I'm entertaining thoughts that don't reflect, and that actually deflect, the creative power I really am.

Ultimately, our bodies allow us to focus on the nature and helpfulness (or lack of it) of our thoughts, as no other element of our experience can. Practice looking at your body as an indicator of your emotional well-being and you'll find yourself appreciating how the process works, and you may even find yourself loving how supportive your body is in helping you refine your focus.

CHAPTER 20

GETTING OUT OF OUR OWN WAY

In reading this far, you may have gotten the impression that I'm making the following claim: that adopting the seer's explanation means that one doesn't have to have 'negative' experiences, or that all will be sweetness and light. I hasten to assure you that the seer's explanation doesn't insulate us from bad feelings, such as anger, resentment, frustration, and all the rest. However, I have found that it does give us a way of considering those feelings when they arise, a way that enables us to allow them to enter our experience from one side and exit out the other.

When we become more keenly aware of what we really don't want, we allow our real Selves to envision and create what we would prefer. The feelings we have when confronting what we *don't* want show us what we *do* want, what will allow us to more fully express ourselves as who we truly are. The story I now tell about myself is that recognizing, allowing, and releasing uncomfortable experiences from the past has enabled me to attract and allow new experiences that I find more joyful.

What follows are two personal stories related from where I now stand.

Finding real success

I was raised by two very competent and accomplished people. Because my father died young, it fell to my mother to do her best to raise me with the values and the understanding about the life she felt would be best for me. Mom was blessed with extraordinary talent, and she was pushed somewhat mercilessly by her father, her first violin teacher, to develop that talent. This she did, with unbending intent and commitment, and she made a real mark on her chosen profession.

My path through life has been quite different from that of my parents. I see my life journey as having a much broader scope, but with much less in the way of tangible accomplishment to show for it. Growing up, I gradually became aware of feelings of confusion and inadequacy as a result of comparing my musical proficiency to that of my parents. 'I,' my Ego, was forced to find ways to make up for that apparent insufficiency.

In my silent comparisons of my mother and myself, I never measured up. In the process, I acquired a misunderstanding of the meaning of success. That misunderstanding, in which I mistook outward expressions for inner realizations, became a deeply ingrained habit, and I believe it has colored many of the interactions I have had with others.

Throughout my musical career, I never felt truly successful. I was always looking in the wrong place, to the external evidence of success that seemed to always be just out of my reach. I now understand that outward indications of success always come about as an expression of the inner knowledge that one is deserving of it. In my experience, expecting to acquire the 'appearance' of success first, in order to allow me the experience of *being* successful, is putting the cart before the horse.

Passive and active acceptance

Recently, I was speaking with my son, who asked about the best way to think about his financial situation in the midst of the current pandemic. His usual income stream had dried up, and, as an independent contractor, he was waiting impatiently for whatever the recent massive stimulus programs might provide for him. Certainly the current situation, as of this writing, requires patience. Many people are now feeling fear, worry, anxiety, and other negative emotions, about their personal situations. We humans typically look at conditions and circumstances that are not the way we want them to be, and we feel that those negative emotions are appropriate and justified as a result.

We often don't notice, however, that the emotions we are feeling are causally related to our thoughts about what is happening to us, or about what's happening out in the world. As soon as we humans start thinking that we're at risk, or that something is 'out to get us,' we start feeling negative emotion no matter what is actually happening in our world.

People who look at scary situations, whether on TV, in a loved one's sick room, or just in their checkbooks, take for granted that it's the situation that's scary. However, according to the seer's explanation, *the situation is just what it is, and it is the thoughts we have about what might happen that are scary*. If fear is a function of thinking we're at risk, then perhaps we can reduce those uncomfortable feelings by finding a better way of thinking about what's going on.

So back to my son's question: what's a better way of thinking about the current economic situation? As he and I talked about it, the question broadened to include not only his financial condition but how to think about what's going on planet wide. I thought about ways of looking at it that would allow us to accept what's happening, as opposed to fighting it. What it finally came down to was understanding a particular kind of acceptance.

I have found that the idea of acceptance can be seen to have two forks, two branches. Those two branches have markedly different results in terms of how we feel about ourselves, in the face of the pandemic or any other significant perceived threat to our well-being. I call those two forks passive and active acceptance.

Passive acceptance is the form of acceptance that is most widely used and understood. Passive acceptance is based on not having any real power over the conditions we face. It implies being resigned to the way things are. It follows from the feeling most of us have, that though we might have wishes, hopes, and desires, we are extremely limited in terms of real power.

We all face unwanted conditions in the form of the actions of other people and the institutions they, and we, create. Your neighbor builds a fence you don't like. The factory upstream dumps something in the environment that negatively impacts the ecosystem that sustains you. Or the government acts in a way as to curtail your sense of personal liberty. There's no shortage of examples of this kind.

When one or more of these conditions is present, and we're unable to persuade those 'others' to change their behavior, we're often told by friends and relatives that we simply have to accept what's happening because we don't actually have the power to make them change. That's what I mean by passive acceptance.

Active acceptance, on the other hand, implies knowing that yes, things are the way they are, but there are possibilities we simply haven't seen yet. If we can just calm down and quiet the noise in our heads, we can listen for hints about what to do or how to think differently about the situation in which we find ourselves.

For example, many people who have lost their jobs during the current pandemic have discovered ways to earn a living at home or to otherwise be creative in how they spend their time. Musicians who can no longer perform in live venues have turned to streaming concerts from their living rooms, giving music lessons online, and engaging in collaborative songwriting. Everyone who desires to re-invent themselves has help available from the Universe. All we need to do is ask, and then watch who shows up to collaborate with us in our mutual reinvention.

Active acceptance is a starting point on the next phase of our journey. We can, if we choose, think of active acceptance as ending one chapter so another can begin. We can think of it as ceasing to resist what we have considered roadblocks or impediments on our path so that we can discover that there is another path with fewer of those roadblocks. We will then know that there is always a way forward, even if we can't see any further than the first turn in the road. The way forward clarifies itself as we stop struggling to control our circumstances. Active acceptance lets us trust our capabilities and our intuition, and it keeps us from succumbing to the resignation of 'Well, I tried' or 'It's just too big for me to handle.'

Maybe we don't have to move our physical selves around nearly as much as we have been, in search of things we want, or jobs that aren't available where we currently are. *Maybe* there are ways to earn a living that we can engage in from our homes, the way many of us feel like we're forced to do now. And *maybe* there are possibilities for us that we couldn't have imagined because we were so focused on the way it's always been done. Perhaps this pandemic-related confinement is all about giving us the chance to take a deep breath and re-imagine our future. What if it's truly about the chance to reinvent ourselves? If you can imagine a future for yourself that makes your heart leap, go there. You won't be disappointed.

Unblocking your power

In an abstract sense, regaining one's power seems as if it should be a simple process: just stop giving it away. But powerlessness is just a story, a story about why you can't have all that your heart desires. And, it's in your way! I have come to see, however, that the people to whom we give our power get attached to having that power. And it appears that they don't want to give it up.

To anyone who wishes to try out that point of view, I suggest setting your boundaries with respect to someone who appears to be in a position of relative power over you. Let them know—lovingly and gently, if possible—that certain of their behaviors, which you formerly had tolerated, are no longer acceptable. Then watch how they react when they realize that you have regained your power over your own life, and they are no longer in control.

CHAPTER 21

METAPHORS TO HELP US
VISUALIZE ALL THIS

The planetarium

When I was young, my dad took me to a planetarium. The theater had a ceiling like a dome, and I sat down in a reclining chair that made it easy to look up. I could see a weird-looking machine in the center of the room that looked kind of like a beetle with a round head and lots of appendages. Someone turned out the lights. Then, I could see on the dome what looked like the night sky, with all the stars and planets. The narrator told us about what those points of light represent and how they move relative to the earth and to one another.

That planetarium was much less sophisticated than those we have today. Even so, it wasn't hard to pretend that each of those points of light I saw on the dome was a separate source of light. But in a planetarium, the same light source powers all of them. And all that movement of points of light relative to one another, and relative to the human in the recliner, is managed by one computer program. That program is designed to tell one story; you could call it the story of the 'heavens.'

The movie we watch on the ceiling when we're comfortably reclined in the planetarium represents the behavior of the physical universe. We humans can make that movie because we have been able to model, in mathematics and in metaphor, all that we perceive 'up there.' Thus, we arrive at what we consider the laws according to which all those 'heavenly' bodies behave.

However, that model of the universe is constructed on top of a foundation which consists of a largely un-noticed belief. We have learned to think of the universe as a mechanical reality devoid of intelligence, caring, and love. We think we see a machine which has no intrinsic purpose, despite our ability to find its representation in the night sky as beautiful, awesome, and compelling. For my part, I have come to believe that the physical universe is far from what I used to think was a lifeless machine.

Metaphorically, the light show on the dome represents the physical universe. But what can we say about the computer program that runs the planetarium? The one that 'knows' how to move each of those points of light in accordance with what we actually observe if we pay attention on clear nights?

That computer program, which I think of as the story of the 'heavens,' represents Universal intelligence. It's the Universe's story, the one we call cosmology, the one that we see portrayed 'on Earth, as it is in Heaven.'

The library

Earlier, I said that our minds record multi-sensory records of the past, and we call these records 'memory.' Those memories also contain the meaning we placed on each of those recorded scenes, as well as a record of the emotions we experienced in those moments of now. And our minds are equipped with a sorting mechanism that allows us to compare the present situation to all those in memory. We then consult our mental library to figure out the action we should take next.

This process is called rationality, or problem-solving using logical analysis. It's a powerful tool when used according to its design. It's like a research library, one that has collected all the works of all its contributors. Scholars look for understanding of the human condition in these stacks, an understanding that will enable them to gain the insights necessary to inform and guide the populace.

The seer's explanation, again, tells us that poring over records of the past won't yield solutions to the problems that, as Einstein said, are caused by the thinking that created them in the first place. Instead, those solutions will be contained in possibilities that we have yet to recognize. Those possibilities must be declared in what Werner Erhard called 'an act of existential courage,' thinking outside the library.

The hard drive and the Internet

I began to build my familiarity with computers and cyberspace in 1979. In those 'distant' days, I could turn on my Apple II, with 48K of RAM memory, input some data, and manipulate that data in some way. If I wanted to store the data, I did so on a floppy disk. This system was extremely limited in its storage capacity, but in 1984, when the IBM PC acquired a hard drive, things were much better. Now I could store lots of data, retrieve it quickly, and search more efficiently for some sought-after answer.

That advancement, from floppy drives to hard drives, was especially useful, but it paled in comparison to that a year or two later when network ports became widely available. One could then connect to that relatively new invention called the Internet. Whereas before I could only search for information on my hard drive, which is to say among those pieces of data that I put there, now the scope of my search had widened immeasurably to those pieces that *everybody* has recorded.

So, when we confine the scope of available information to our past, to the library, we are limited to what's on our metaphorical hard drives. And that has us repeating over and over the actions of the past, perhaps with changes of names and places but with no real progress toward any of our visions.

Why don't we just enable our 'network ports' and draw from a vastly larger storehouse of ideas? The seer's explanation says *it is our belief in separation that keeps us from doing so.* Where do we localize our thought process? We say, 'it's in my head.' We are totally committed to the idea that consciousness is one of the attributes of this physical body, and to the idea that our bodies represent our Selves and are separated in physical space. So, it's hard for us to imagine that we might be connected, let alone that we might actually be One with each other and with the Universe.

The orchestra

To understand this metaphor, I believe we have to start with Source, pure Being, pure awareness, All-that-Is. In terms of the seer's explanation, *pure awareness is the context, that which contains everything else.* Within that context there is Mind, which contains all the thoughts and combinations of thoughts that have ever been thought. In the mind, all those thoughts "float like barges," as Juan Matus put it.

We can think of all those thoughts as vibrations or vibrational modes of an invisible field. You can visualize this field as a vast orchestra playing an unimaginably complex piece of music. The air in the equally vast auditorium vibrates according to all these rich tones, with each instrument uniquely characterized by an immediately identifiable sound. Our ears and brains then turn that immense collection of vibrational patterns into, first sound, and then what we think of as a symphony.

In terms of those vibrations, each of us humans hears, sees, and feels a unique combination of those vibrational modes. And like televisions, each of us has the ability to tune in, decode, and interpret those vibrations. That interpretation places on the screen of life the sights and sounds of a multi-sensory picture that seems so real we take it to be our ultimate reality. We call that process of interpretation, 'perception.' According to the seer's explanation, *perception is an act of creation and not simply one of observing.*

The assemblage point

Earlier I spoke of the assemblage point, that unique combination of frequencies at which each of us metaphorically vibrates. The assemblage point is the specific group of vibrations from which we assemble the world we perceive.

I spoke about *hearing* that combination of vibrations, as if I'm tuning into my favorite radio station. I have discovered I can also *feel* the position of my assemblage point. That point, the frequency at which I choose to vibrate, determines the quality of life that I experience.

I believe there is a sweet spot for each of us, a position that is personally ideal. If we stop resisting the way things are and trust that Spirit, All-That-Is, has everything well in hand, our assemblage points will progressively gravitate to that spot. And it is truly sweet.

The street gang

The seer's explanation says: *as individual expressions of pure consciousness, we made a deliberate tradeoff to come here.* What we got is the richness of physical experience. What we traded for that, willingly and temporarily, is the memory of who we *really* are. We, as the Self, chose to come here to Earth, and we wound up identifying with the invented, separate, limited self. We allowed the Ego to obscure our true Selves. Practically speaking, we *became* the Ego.

As we live in the explanation we inherited from our culture, we tend to feel the feelings associated with being separate, limited creatures. These feelings consist of anxiety, frustration, and fear, the negative feelings we all feel at one time or another, and to one degree or another. And so, this world becomes for us a battleground, a stressful and sometimes violent 'neighborhood' in which we strive to maximize our competitive edge, amassing the symbols of success and security, and minimizing the risks we believe to be inherent in our neighborhood and in this 'game' of life.

How can we visualize this 'neighborhood' we're speaking about, that has us acting contrary to our own interests and is indifferent to our true well-being? It's like a 'street gang,' in that adherence to the gang's ethos and language is the trade-off for the protection and belonging that the gang offers. We have no choice but to buy into all this, and it does provide some measure of stability and predictability to our lives.

However, the protection and belonging are illusory. Gangs don't actually protect members from violence and death. And our cultural understanding certainly doesn't protect us from pain and suffering. In fact, our shared explanation of life appears to doom us to lives of frustration, trying to protect ourselves from others and from undesired conditions. That's what gives rise to fences, and walls, and nuclear missiles.

What's the way out of this oppressive invention, this Ego-gang? The way out is the same as the way out of any superstition. You recognize it as a superstition. When you finally understand that black cats aren't *really* bad luck, you may still flinch when one crosses your path, but you can remind yourself that the connection between the animal and some potentially bad future experience isn't real. And then, over time, you can alter your response to the cat, just as you can with the 'street gang.'

The bubble

As one does this work of separating superstitions from reality, we see ourselves traveling along a path of increasing recognition that the power of the mass cultural understanding is an illusion. As I do that, I experience what I call living in 'the bubble.'

The bubble is like a safety zone, and it's also like an empowerment zone. It's the space in which I experience life. And it's like the horizon in that it isn't dependent on the geography of my physical landscape. It goes with me, because like the horizon, it's a function of perception.

A couple of years ago, we decided to take this idea 'on the road,' and find out if we could have the experience of being in the bubble 'out there,' among the fast-food joints, and the crowded cities and heavy traffic, and among people who strongly hold viewpoints that we might not share.

Well, sometimes the beds were better than others, and sometimes the places we stayed were cleaner than others. Sometimes the food we were served was ordinary, and sometimes it was wonderful. But we always felt comfortable, like we were being taken care of while given opportunities to further explore what we like and what we don't like.

But what *is* that bubble? How does it work? How could we visualize it? Most importantly, how can we use the bubble metaphor to enhance our experience of life? And how can I speak about it so that someone else can feel that way about wherever they are?

In the books of Carlos Castaneda, Juan Matus describes that bubble like this:

> We are inside a bubble. It is a bubble into which we are placed at the moment of our birth. At first the bubble is open, but then it begins to close until it has sealed us in. The bubble is our perception. We live inside that bubble all our lives. And what we witness on its round walls is our own reflection. The thing reflected is our view of the world. That view is first a description which is given to us from the moment of our birth until all our attention is caught by it and the description becomes a view.[9]

So, we can think of ourselves as living in a bubble. So what? Is the idea to get rid of the bubble? No, none of us is going to 'pop the world'! That possibility isn't available to us. But if you think about popping a bubble, you're thinking that there's something outside that bubble, which will be seen or revealed when the bubble is gone. But the bubble is everything. It's our world! So, if this is not about getting rid of the bubble, then what's the value of this metaphor?

---

[9] Carlos Castaneda, *Tales of Power* (New York: Simon and Schuster, 1974), 246-247.

Well, if your story, your view, has become your world, and if we each create our own reality, then we're each in our own bubble, looking 'out' at a reflection of our own ideas. So here we are, floating around, occasionally bumping into one another... and because we share a description of reality, we can talk to one another and share experiences.

But we *forget* we're each in our own bubble, and we think we have the power to negatively affect one another's experience. So, we feel guilt. And we think others have the power to affect our experience, to get in the way of our hopes and dreams, our goals and intentions. So, we feel fear, or some other negative emotion that we either act out in some defensive manner or hide from others.

However, those negative feelings depend on the assumption that we're all in the same bubble, like the bubble is a real dome! If I think of myself as living in a bubble of my own creation, and that everyone else does as well, I can avoid a tremendous waste of energy. Blame goes away, as does resentment, embarrassment, and all the other negative emotions we associate with living around other people. Because each of us creates our own story, the story reflected by our own bubbles!

The helix (the slinky)

The helix is the shape of a coiled spring. When it's collapsed, it is essentially a circle, a two-dimensional object. Picture this device lying on a flat surface. It just seems to go around and around. However, when you stretch it, you are doing so into an additional dimension. In our metaphor of the slinky or the coiled spring, that third dimension is called 'up.'

I have already introduced the helix as a metaphor for expanded understanding. Life keeps bringing me back around to the same life issues, but each time I see them from a broader perspective. The metaphor of the helix points to gradually increasing understanding of the lessons that life repeatedly offers us. The 'up' dimension into which the helix is stretched points to the breadth of perspective. The higher the level on the helix, the broader the perspective.

Now let's consider the possibility of looking from the perspective of the helix at one's life, as well as at the life of all the humans on the planet and the organism we call Earth. If you think of the helix as standing with its base, its first circle, sitting on the floor, then each time you go around the circle you are looking down at your past from a somewhat higher perspective. Please note that my use of the word 'higher' does not refer to a moral scale. It's simply a broader perspective, like the one you would gain as you climbed the ramp of a parking garage while looking out over the city.

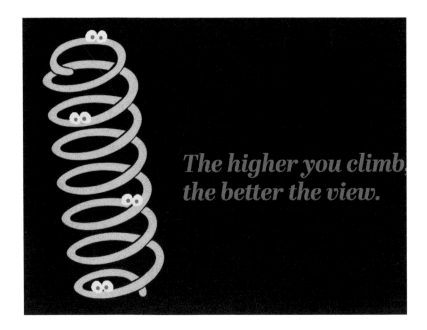

The higher you climb, the better the view.

Now, as you climb, you see that you and everybody else are just where you and they are on the helix. In this sense, none of us is better or smarter than anyone else. It's just that your perspective improves. The cityscape you can see from the parking garage can represent the state of the world. Down on the lower levels, it doesn't look so good. All we can see from down there is building facades, some of which might be decrepit and greatly in need of repair. We might see a pile of trash or some other blight, and the effect on us might be negative. We might be irritated, frustrated, or even angry or afraid.

However, as we continue to climb, we are increasingly able to see the design of the city itself. First, we might note how the neighborhood is laid out, then how the neighborhoods interface with one another, and eventually how the whole city is laid out. There is actually beauty in those patterns!

Because we are enmeshed in the Ego, the cultural understanding we all share, we might come to feel that our broader perspective makes us somewhat better, or more advanced, than those below us on the parking garage ramp. Similarly, we may fall into the trap of considering ourselves less advanced than those above us on the helix. And here we are, back in the Ego's vicious circle of comparison and competition.

Again, the way out is to remember that the power of the Ego is a superstition, and that we're all One. Each of us represents a different perspective on the Universe, and it requires all perspectives to get a complete picture of All-That-Is. We don't each occupy one place on the helix; each of us *is* the helix! We each have the ability to expand our own helix so that each turn affords a significantly better view.

Breadcrumbs

In Joni Mitchell's classic song, 'Woodstock,' there is the line, "and we've got to get ourselves back to the Garden." In that line, I hear her profound desire to return to a state of Being in which all negative feelings have been released and true peace is regained. Allow me to offer my take on how we might 'get back' to that state of grace.

As we let our internal dialog die down, and as we experience our world in that silence, thoughts arise. If we pay attention, we can see that each of these thoughts has feeling associated with it. The emotional content can be so slight we don't notice it, but it is still there. However, when we have ascribed sufficient meaning to a thought, we feel a strong feeling. That feeling is a function of whether it is an appealing or unappealing thought.

Let's be clear about this use of 'good' and 'bad.' In the seer's explanation, that distinction is not moral; *morality lives in the domain of interpretation and not in reality*. Instead, the good/bad distinction lives in the realm of feeling, and every person knows when thoughts feel good or bad, though we typically collapse that distinction and say that it's *we* who feel good or bad.

Bad-feeling thoughts are rooted in the conventional explanation with its inclusion of the ideas of limitation, scarcity, inevitability, and so on. And good-feeling thoughts are rooted in pure Being-ness, in who we really are. Follow those good-feeling thoughts. They are the 'breadcrumbs' with which we can find our way back, to who we really are, to the Garden. Breadcrumbs? You'll have fun looking up that reference, as I did! Hansel and Gretel, and the Brothers Grimm.

CHAPTER 22

IN SUMMARY: WHAT IS A HUMAN BEING, REALLY?

In chapter 2, we asked ourselves a question that most of us have never heard, let alone thought about: 'What is a human being, anyway?' Whatever answer pops into your mind, it probably involves an object, namely a human body, with attributes, such as size and shape, and with faculties, such as senses, thoughts, and feelings.

It's my hope that in these pages you have found the inspiration to consider a much larger possibility for the Being of human beings. Accordingly, I will use this chapter to summarize that argument as clearly as I am able.

Common sense

All of us are familiar with an *idea* of human being. We use that term with a sense that we know what it refers to. First, we reviewed the usual definition of the term, in order to see if it is supported by what I call bedrock science, principles that have proven their ability to explain what we see. We concluded that it is not. Let's review and restate.

Starting our inquiry into the true nature of human-ness, I discussed 'what everybody knows,' sometimes referred to by the term 'common sense.' Common sense implies that there exists a body of common understanding underneath all of the ideas about which we debate and often disagree.

WE SEE EVERYTHING WE LOOK AT THROUGH AN OCEAN OF HIDDEN AS-SUMPTIONS

You may recall my fish story from the introduction. The fish doesn't see the water itself, but if the water is clouded or colored, the color or cloudiness affects his view of whatever he's looking at, because he sees everything *through* the water. Regarding common sense, we say first that the way we see the world is shaped or colored by our belief systems. We don't see our belief systems; they are transparent to us. That is to say, we don't see our world view; we just see the world through it. When we use the saying 'It's like water to the fish,' that's what we mean. So common sense, that which we never examine, is the water we swim in. It's 'what we all know.'

Refer back to the symbol of 'flat earth' to represent how people commonly saw the world many generations ago. Let's have it represent all the things that we humans once believed but have now discarded because science, or our other intellectual pursuits, convinced us that there's a better way of looking at things. Most of us consider a view like 'flat earth' to be primitive.

Also, common sense always lags behind scientific understanding. We experience something that doesn't fit our belief system, and we think about it, or even experiment with it, and eventually we say, "Yeah, that's really true!" The earth really is round! And *then* we can discard the 'what everybody knows' about the earth being flat.

Is it possible that we 'moderns' believe in stuff that isn't real? To get a start with that question, we first explored the crucial difference between how something appears and what it actually is.

Superstition revisited

Let's revisit the word 'superstition.' It points to the confusion between something that's *believed* to be real but isn't, and that which *is* real. Superstitions can have power over us, but only when they're not understood to be superstitions, but are rather thought to be truths. If you don't know that some idea is a superstition, your belief in the reality of that idea can and often will affect your range of possible choices.

So we ask, "What superstitions might now cloud or color the water we swim in?" Because if there are superstitions embedded in our world view, they *will* affect whatever we look at through that world view.

Underneath all our beliefs is something virtually *all* of us believe: the world we perceive would be there if all of us were to disappear. We believe that the world is pretty much the way we perceive it to be.

That which we think is real, I call an 'is.' We humans believe that the world is an 'is.' So, there *is* a world out there whose existence is independent of our presence in it. Now, is that belief true? Or is it a superstition?

First, let's look for a solid, scientific basis for the belief that the world is an 'is.' Let's make this belief tangible for ourselves. Imagine, if you will, a piece of furniture that's made of wood. Let's test what we might call the 'is-ness' of this object. What's the wood made of? I looked it up, and the primary component of wood is cellulose. Ok, what's the cellulose made of? The Internet 'tells' me that it's made of molecules containing certain kinds of atoms. You can, if you like, pull up a diagram of the molecular structure of cellulose.

So far so good.

If you now ask what those atoms are made of, and if you want to do some bedrock science about them, the answers start to get much less understandable. It turns out that when you want to analyze atoms you have to use quantum theory. Quantum theory gives you reliable, experimentally verifiable answers to any appropriate question you might ask of it. But quantum theory also says some very strange things, some very non-intuitive things about the world. See Chapter 8 if you want to brush up on them.

The bottom line is that quantum theory flatly contradicts the idea that we are observers of a world that exists independently of whether or not we observe it. And quantum theory definitely doesn't fit with common sense, or 'what everybody knows.'

So, I made a statement that almost every human mind will instantly reject: the existence of the world as an 'is' is a superstition as well. If you really consider what quantum theory tells us, I think you'll realize that the world isn't an 'is,' but is rather what we might call an 'appears as,' like the horizon that appears to be an edge off of which you could fall. The world *appears* to be permanent and stable. And it *appears* to be real. But so did the edge that mariners used to see when they looked at the horizon and were afraid of falling off it. The existence of that edge turned out to be a superstition.

Common sense and human Being

What is the 'what everybody knows' about the term 'human being'? Classically speaking, a human being is "a man, woman, or child of the species homo sapiens, distinguished from other animals by superior mental development, power of articulate speech, and upright stance," according to one typical definition.

You could say that this idea of human being is object-oriented. We tend to think of ourselves as objects against the background of the world. It's an object-oriented definition of human being and it fits perfectly with the Ego, the invented self, which is a product of the cultural understanding I spoke of earlier. One of the problems with the object-oriented view of human beings is that it locks us into separation and limitation, competition and inevitability.

The quantum viewpoint, on the other hand, allows us to overcome the idea of separation through something called non-locality. Locality is an idea in physics to denote that each object has a separate location. Our belief in that idea is essentially absolute. But in terms of our *experience*, how many locations are there? There is only one: 'here.' It's impossible to *experience* any other location than 'here.' Everywhere else is abstract and intangible. Everywhere else lives in interpretation, in our story. In this view, there aren't any separate locations. Not *really*!

Non-locality, the absence of real separate locations, is a demonstrable result of carefully controlled experiments in physics that have been done for over a hundred years. Quantum physics has established that non-locality is a fundamental principle of the world. But it radically violates common sense. Our idea that objects such as our bodies *are* located in real, separate locations doesn't hold up under the scrutiny of quantum physics!

The existence of objects where we find them, including our bodies, is literally a product of observation, *by us*. Everything about bodies, including their existence where we find them, is a product of observation. That makes it hard to cling to the idea that we *are* our bodies. How could something that requires observation to exist, do the observing that's required?

A new fundamental assumption about human beings

Ok, so if an object-based definition of human being doesn't work, what does? So far, this summary of the seer's explanation has followed a fairly logical path. Any logical argument must start with at least one supposition. The problem is that the foundation upon which we traditionally base our entire world view is hidden. So, at least, we should make our new logical argument on top of an assumption that's *visible*.

Again, we have built our prevailing interpretation of the world's appearance on top of the idea that the world is an 'is,' and that it provides the context or container in which we humans come and go. By contrast, the assumption on top of which the seer's explanation rests is that consciousness is the true container, that it *is* and always was, and it is One, indivisible. Everything else is a function of that One consciousness and has its existence *within it*. So, we must, in our most essential nature, *be* that consciousness. In my experience, that consciousness is all-knowing and all-loving. I call that one loving being Spirit, or the Universe, All-That-Is, or simply, the Self.

So, we arrive at a potential, trial definition of 'human being': a human being is that aspect of All-That-Is, of Spirit, that brings one of many possible worlds from the quantum field into actuality. Now, let's see where that might take us.

The quantum field

Let us review this idea of the quantum field. First, so we're on the same page, one of the most basic ideas in physics is that of the field. Fields are thought of as occupying all of space, and they're thought of as having the capacity at each point in space to affect objects in that location.

We can't see fields. They're not tangible or directly observable. They're abstract, but you can experience their effects. For example, we're all familiar with the gravitational field. We can't see it, but it exists at all points in space, and it has the capacity to affect objects at each location. You don't need to understand the gravitational field. Just fall down a couple of times and you'll know all you need to know.

You've probably also encountered a magnetic field, if you've used a compass or played with a magnet and a bunch of iron filings. And there's the electric field, which you can experience if you rub a balloon on your sweater and then hold it next to your hair.

Another point about fields: as far as I know, all fields can sustain vibrations, or waves, much like those on the surface of a pond if you throw a rock into it. And those vibrations automatically propagate or spread out. For example, propagating vibrations of the electromagnetic field are called light.

And a final point: these vibrations once created, as 'starlight' for example, never die out. The light we see coming from stars at night left those stars millions or billions of years ago. The vibrations just keep on going forever, and they always will.

Ok, we've reacquainted ourselves with the field as an idea. Now we can talk specifically about the quantum field. I'd like to introduce you to Amit Goswami. He's a theoretical physicist, actually my favorite. Here's a quote from him:

> Quantum physics is the physics of possibilities. And not just material possibilities, but also possibilities of meaning, of feeling, and of intuiting. You choose everything you experience from these possibilities, so quantum physics is a way of understanding your life as one long series of choices that are in themselves the ultimate acts of creativity.[10]

As a way of visualizing something that's as abstract and intangible as could be, we can think of all these possibilities as vibrations in the quantum field. And in this quotation, Goswami speaks about choosing a vibration from the quantum field, just like tuning your radio to one frequency out of all the frequencies at which the electromagnetic field is vibrating in your vicinity.

Once again, the quantum field is abstract; we can't see it, but we can experience its effects. That infinitude of possibilities exists at each point in space (and time), and those possibilities

---

[10] https://www.azquotes.com/author/38915-Amit_Goswami

never die out. I've heard it said that once a thought or an idea is conceived, it will always exist.

Now, does the quantum field affect us, the way these other fields do? Yes, but the quantum field appears to be different in that it is *we* who exert its effects, rather than the field itself. This is where it's useful to recall the film theater analogy I spoke of earlier. Every time we tell our story (the film strip), we select one possible world, one possible arrangement of all the symbols of which our world consists. And that possibility, over time, comes to be reflected back to us by the 'screen' of the quantum field.

Human beings and freedom

The seer's explanation leads to a discussion about the distinction between 'freedom from' and 'freedom to.' Here are some dictionary definitions of freedom. And I recommend you notice that all these definitions of 'freedom' place freedom at one end of a scale, the other end of which is some sort of bondage or limitation. Freedom, in this context, is:

- The state of being free or at liberty rather than in confinement or under physical restraint.
- Exemption from external control, interference, regulation, etc.
- The power to determine action without restraint.

I call that kind of freedom, 'freedom from.' It's freedom in the context of duality. Duality is the hallmark of thinking and being inside of an object-oriented definition of 'human being,' and it's the signature of the Ego. And what do you get in duality? You get a pendulum. A pendulum swings back and forth. The harder you push it to one side, the more forcefully it swings to the other side. In duality nothing is ever really achieved. There's just movement back and forth, back and forth.

So maybe that's not really freedom!

What is freedom then? Well, as Amit Goswami said, "[You can understand] your life as one long series of choices that are in themselves the ultimate acts of creativity."

The seer's explanation says that *freedom is choosing your own story from the infinitude of possibilities and knowing that you have the power to actualize that story in your experience.* It's the freedom to say "no" to your conditioning that makes you mechanical and pre-determined, to say "no" to the constraints self-imposed by your beliefs. It's the freedom to say "yes" to whatever your heart desires. It's 'freedom to.' And *that* freedom doesn't live in duality. It's who you really are!

Now, an important question flows from this new awareness of the quantum field of possibilities: 'If the quantum field includes *all* possibilities, how can I enlarge *my* field of possibilities? How do I go about accessing more of what's in the quantum field?'

To answer that question, we introduced another metaphor: the evolution of the computer. The first personal computer didn't have a network connection or network port. If you needed an answer, what you could search through for that answer was only what you as an individual user put there.

Nowadays, all computers have network ports, and all are 'aware' of the Internet. What you can search through is what *all* users have put there, in all times, and in all places. This Internet metaphor reminds us that all possibilities that Spirit has ever imagined are available to each of us to actualize; all it requires is our focused attention and our willingness to look for additional possibilities beyond the box which has always contained our thoughts. We walk around thinking that we have to make the best decisions we can based on our own experience. The seer's explanation tells us that *we have access to all the experience that all of us have ever had! And not just those of us alive now.*

Do we really create our own reality?

What does 'you create your own reality' really mean? Let's first recognize that you don't create your own reality from the 'ground up,' from nothing. If you did, you'd have to create it starting with atoms and molecules and other things which are vibrational in nature … and none of us knows how to do that, at least not on a human scale. Fortunately, we don't have to 'recreate the wheel,' because when we come forth into this time-space reality, we are showing up in an already-established platform that incorporates certain rules, including the laws of physics and the human template I referred to in chapter 2.

So, you don't create your reality from nothing. In a sense, you create it from everything, by ignoring, disbelieving, or filtering out everything to the contrary. Let's go back to our television set. The physical cable that the cable company gives you contains all the programs you could possibly watch. To actually watch a program, however, you have to tune the TV to a particular frequency. The TV has to essentially tune out or disregard everything else. Most of us are unaware that we have done the same thing with the infinitude of possibilities in the quantum field, due to our acceptance of what everybody knows.

To exist within the human community, we have to focus on the possibility we've chosen to the exclusion of all other possibilities. Everyone who has ever lived on planet Earth has accomplished that maneuver. It's what we call humanity. And in the process, the possibilities of human experience we have chosen to disregard are without limit.

CHAPTER 23

THE EVOLUTION
OF HUMAN BEING

A new definition of Ego

Let's talk again about Ego. I use that word to label our cultural understanding of the self, which we 'buy into' in order to play in this reality 'game.' In one sense, it's like a 'piece' we use to play a board game like Monopoly. Let's say you're playing that game, and you roll the dice or draw a chance card that puts your piece on a square. Perhaps that square calls for consequences, such as 'Go directly to jail.'

Now ask yourself: does that consequence apply to you (your Self), or to your piece (yourself)? It seems clear that it applies to your piece! Since you know you're playing Monopoly, *you* don't feel incarcerated. However, for most of us in this 'game' of life, the consequences of the 'chance' cards are very real. We all forget that we're playing a game, and so we *experience* the incarceration and describe it as loss of freedom.

Now let's ask, what is the effect upon us of identifying with the 'piece,' the Ego-self? I think of that *identification* as destructive to our experience of well-being. It separates us from our true nature, which is oneness with each other and with All-That-Is. In doing so, it forces us to believe in scarcity, danger, evil, and inevitability. All these beliefs, which require forgetting who we truly are, result in mass human behavior that is completely contrary to our best interests. And who or what is being served in the process? It is the Ego itself.

If we wish to experience the freedom that is our birthright, what is demanded of us is to break free of the Ego, to recognize it as an invention whose 'power' is a superstition. What we have to do is drive a wedge between the Ego, the invented self, and who we really are. However, that 'remedy' makes it sound as if the Ego is the 'bad guy' and must somehow be gotten rid of. I believe that is too narrow a view.

Let's postulate that what is thought of as the evolution of species isn't simply the mechanism of natural selection, or survival of the fittest. Let's consider the possibility that Spirit, *the conscious Universe*, has spent the last 14 billion years or so experimenting, trying out new ideas. The overall arc of this experimentation has been towards *more fully expressing Spirit, the pure energy of creation, Itself*. Let's consider the further possibility that homo sapiens, our species, is the current state of that ongoing experiment in how best to express in the world the fullness that is Spirit!

Well, where are we going *from here*? At first blush, that question might sound as strange as wondering what superstitions we might still be operating within. The hubris, the arrogance of thinking that we human beings are as good as it gets, might be blinding us to what else is possible.

What is homo sapiens? The first phrase of the classic definition is 'superior mental development.' In light of all that I have presented thus far, I think this component of the definition can be reworded as 'superior development of rationality and problem-solving.'

If we stand on this definition, what do we see looking down the road into our possible futures? I think it may well be that homo sapiens is reaching the end of the line. Homo sapiens, the master of rationality and logical thinking, cannot solve the problems it faces. To paraphrase Albert Einstein, you can't solve problems with the same kind of thinking that created them.

Is this bad news? It certainly sounds like it. But ...

The asteroid of our times

Imagine yourself one of the biggest, 'baddest' dinosaurs about 66 million years ago. There you are, king of the world, having perfected 'dominant' and 'predator' without any meaningful challengers. And then one day, here comes this giant asteroid, and the next day its impact with the earth has made your life ultimately impossible. You have no way of evolving, and so you perish. And in so doing you make room for the rise of mammals and, eventually, us.

In the current version of the story about that asteroid, its effect upon Earth was planet-wide. You can think of the results of that impact as being present everywhere in the biosphere and having the capability of affecting every object within its scope. Just like those invisible fields we spoke of earlier.

I'm proposing that we think of the Ego as just such a field. It's 'the water we swim in,' and everyone is looking at life through it. It's planet-wide, because each and every human culture has a few fundamental, invisible beliefs at its core. One such widely held belief is that we are separate beings, separate from one another and from Spirit. And the belief that we're all on our own, together with the belief in scarcity, dooms us to conflict and competition. If you read or watch the news, you will see the effect of that Egoic field upon us humans and our institutions, and *you will see it everywhere.*

It seems to me that the pandemic of 2020, which in that year was practically all we heard about, has stripped bare the global Ego, revealing its true nature.

The global Ego pictures us as separate, vulnerable creatures faced with an invisible enemy (in this case, the virus) that is taking over the planet, and we feel as if we have no choice but to fight, and resist, and defend. Our leaders, irrespective of party or ideology, feel compelled to lead us in the fight against that invisible enemy, or at least to give us the impression that they are doing all they can or should do to defend us against it. However, they are fundamentally conflicted, because the Ego also demands of them that they be right in their ideas and pronouncements, even if they have no idea what they are talking about.

President Trump served us by showing us the logical extreme of that inner conflict. He is, or at least has said he is, distrustful of science and scientists. Furthermore, he has championed the 'common man' in that average person's distrust of the scientific 'elite.' However, as the 'leader of the free world,' he was compelled to provide us with answers, inadequate though they were, about how to deal with the pandemic. Complicating that picture further is his need to be loved, to be looked up to, and to have the approval of enough of us to be reelected. It's an impossible role he took on, all dictated by the way the world looks to him through the Egoic field, the water he swims in.

With all that in mind, another way to think about that Egoic field is as a giant asteroid. Suppose the design function of that field, that 'asteroid,' is to bring about the evolution of the entire biosphere, us included. Let's see how that would look.

The design function of the Ego

Earlier, I said that the news isn't just information. In our culture it is always prepared and presented from the point of view of a particular explanation. Newscasts are prepared from within a specific view of the world, and they are delivered from that perspective. The news, whether it's left, right, or center, can be seen as the mouthpiece of the global Ego. And I'm convinced that the way the Ego actually functions *is to perpetuate itself.*

The global Ego, and the understanding of the world that created it, makes itself indispensable to us. How does it do that? I will say here again—and over and over in general—that the world we perceive isn't an 'is.' The world we perceive is, instead, an interpretation or description rather than the world itself, which, to quote Juan Matus once again, is 'mysterious and unfathomable.' What makes the world real for us is our resistance to it.

Wait ... how does *that* work?

Let's say you're standing in a mountain stream, facing upstream, and just enjoying the flow of the clear, cold water. You can take a drink, you can wash yourself, or you can just stand there in pure delight. But look, coming towards you is a clump of something floating on the surface of the stream. The closer it gets, the worse it smells.

What do you do? Do you grab it and express your disgust? If you do, now it's all over your hands! But if you just let it go, it floats on downstream, and you can return to your joyful reverie. I have found that if I just let the world be, it will let me be. The moment I react to something unwanted, that unwanted thing tends to stick around and then I have to deal with it over and over until I release it. We humans are not letting the world be, we're fighting it and each other, and it (the world) won't let us be, either.

I think this logical argument leads to the following conclusion: the global Ego has essentially enslaved us, it has insured that we will do its bidding by pitting us against one another, and it is really only interested in its own survival. I said earlier that for us individual humans, the strategies we adopted in trying to ensure our own survival seem to become strategies for the survival of the mind itself. This is the same argument on a global scale.

The global Ego as meteorology

Meteorology is "a branch of the atmospheric sciences which includes atmospheric chemistry and physics, with a major focus on weather forecasting." Earlier, when I described physics in the 20th century, I pointed out that it was once believed that with enough time, effort, and computing power, one could extrapolate from knowing how atoms and molecules interact with each other to understanding the weather.

Meteorologists, however, know that is a hopeless task. Far more fruitful is the consideration of weather as a global system. This realization leads me to consider that the behavior of human societies is best understood from this same large-scale perspective and not from the extrapolation of individual human interactions. The global Ego I propose is just such a system, and from that perspective, we can think of planet-wide disruptions in human affairs in the same terms as climate change.

What is happening to Earth's climate seems likely to force human adaptation on a massive scale. This will probably range from changes in individual behavior, to the development of new technologies to compensate for uncontrollable changes, to the uprooting of entire communities. It is in this sense that I believe the global Ego, which seems equally uncontrollable, will force us to adapt, or more accurately, to evolve.

The evolution of human Being

Individual human beings generally prefer peace to war and wellbeing to suffering. From that perspective, it's difficult to understand why war and poverty persist. Aren't we just a large number of people making decisions in our own best interest? No, not if we have given over our choices to those of a global system which has its own agenda. No, not if that agenda is its own survival, its own indispensability!

I have portrayed the global Ego as a system of oppression in which we humans find ourselves here on Earth. However, we are Spirit in human form. We *chose* to come here to participate in this drama, with great purpose, from a place of complete knowing. Why would we do that if we knew that we would be enslaved in this manner?

First of all, the opportunity to have real life experience is a powerful draw. Esther Hicks speaks of the strong human desire to get our 'hands in the clay.' But beyond that, I believe we all feel the desire to participate somehow in the creation of a better story about the world. So, there was a broader, more powerful draw to come to Earth and to the global Ego. It was to participate in the evolution of human Being from homo sapiens to whatever is next. And this evolution requires revealing and then dispensing with the superstition that we *are* the Ego.

When that occurs, the Ego, the invented self, will reveal itself to be a creation of our acculturation and not the reality of who we really are. Then we will find within ourselves the willingness to forsake the payoffs of our collective racket and free ourselves. Remember, the racket is a masquerade, a 'dishonest scheme' by which we show others who we think we need to be.

When we free ourselves from our masquerade, we will take back our power and become fully aware of the truth of who we really are. We will *consciously* become the Self, a painter who applies the paint to the canvas of the world, a poet who paints a picture with his or her words and makes it into real experience. That is what we are witnessing right now: early signs of the evolution of the human Being.

If you consider that possibility, you may see, as I do, that we are watching not only the evolution of our species but also of the entire biosphere. Homo sapiens is boxed in by our identification with an oppressive cultural Ego. As homo sapiens, our time is up. However, our evolution doesn't require getting rid of the Ego; in fact, we can't. We simply must rid ourselves of our *identification* with that Ego and stop thinking that's who we are!

Let me hasten to add that this 'asteroid' is different. It's different in that the dinosaurs were unable to evolve into something that would be consistent with a world more reflective of Spirit expressing Itself. In particular, they had to disappear so as to allow the rise of the mammals. We homo sapiens, on the other hand, *can* evolve. Our evolution doesn't require a different branch of the animal kingdom, or better bodies, bigger brains, and so on. It only requires that we become clear about the distinction between our Being and the image of ourselves held in the Ego. We are not separate members of a competitive species. We are all the same Spirit in human bodies.

CHAPTER 24

SO, WHAT'S NEXT?

Surviving the 'asteroid'

We're almost there. We have seen how the seer's explanation offers us an opportunity to extricate ourselves from our fundamental superstitions and remember who we are. And yet, you may find yourself with nagging doubts.

You may be entertaining questions such as, 'How can I possibly feel that free in the context of what I see on the news every day? How can I possibly feel that good, knowing as I do that so many other human beings are living in poverty, disease, and war? And how can I feel true well-being in the face of the impacts I personally feel from various economic, social, and medical conditions?'

It is time to wake up within what is effectively a lucid dream and remember who and what we really are. And I believe we must. I believe that we are being urged, with increasing firmness by the impact of the 'asteroid of our time,' to evolve into what might be referred to as 'homo spiritus.' Homo spiritus is human beings knowing in our heart of hearts that we are One, eternal, loved without condition, and ultimately free to create, unrestrained and without limit, according to our heart's desire. Knowing in the depth of our hearts that we are Spirit in human form—and thus all equal, all One—makes us members of that brand new species, that which our 'asteroid' is designed to bring about.

We must remember that, unlike the dinosaurs whose bodies could not survive the new era ushered in by the asteroid, we are not being asked to evolve our bodies. You can think of that asteroid 66 million years ago as having demanded that the dinosaurs adapt to the new conditions. And that, they were unable to do. But we are being asked only to adapt our understanding of who we are: the Self, and not the self. *And that we can do.* Let me see if I can tell you a story that will illustrate that possibility for you.

"All the world's a stage" -- Shakespeare

Imagine your Self with some aspect of human experience or behavior that you would like to explore. Let's say that you have chosen to produce a play, a drama, in order to illustrate a theme, or perhaps the interaction or collision between a couple of themes.

What elements do you need to assemble for this play? Well, you will need a stage. You will need actors, and you'll need a script. The actors should be able to put their own personalities aside and immerse themselves in the roles you've written for them. The script will be a story that will illustrate the theme you chose, and it will allow the actors to develop their roles.

So, you secure a playhouse with its stage for rehearsals and eventual production. You hire actors that you trust for their professionalism and their capabilities. You also need to develop a script. But wait … maybe the actors are accomplished enough to work out a script as they go. That would be more efficient, because then the writers don't have to convince the actors that what they've written makes sense and is worth performing. More importantly, it will provide the actors with an opportunity to really exercise their creativity.

Give them a theme, a role, a purpose, or some other abstraction to work with, and let them interact with one another, like improv! The actors will generate the dialog and the movements themselves as they go.

Now, shift your perspective on all this. Allow yourself to imagine that someone else, a fine actor, is playing you, your self. That actor started with a premise presented by the director, interacted with other such actors, and allowed the dialog and the action to follow naturally. Your story is most interesting (it really *is*, by the way). The actor who plays you really wanted to see how it would turn out if your theme were allowed to unfold organically, so that actor chose willingly to immerse him or herself in the role of you as completely as possible, even to the point of losing themselves in the role. They forgot they were just playing a part.

Now ask yourself, what's the difference between that imagined scenario and what's going on now, in your 'real life'? Imagine that you yourself are a great actor, and you are totally committed to your part. You (your Self) took on a premise of your choosing, and you lost yourself in the role of a person you invented. And that act of forgetting who you really are, that voluntary amnesia, allows you to fully engage your creativity and immerse yourself in the role of you, completely.

Let's see how the world looks from that perspective.

Choose a particular scenario so we can flesh this out. For example, suppose that you, the actor, want to explore what it's like to be lonely. Perhaps, more specifically, you want to explore the scarcity of potential lovers. An appropriate premise might be that available members of the desired gender are rare in your town, or in your social class, or within your circle of friends. Sometimes this is expressed as, 'All the good ones are taken.'

In order to express that perspective—the scarcity of potential lovers—on stage, the character of you might behave in such a way that the other characters in whom you might be interested will not gather around you in significant numbers. Or they might behave as if you were not particularly desirable yourself. Or they might behave as they would if they weren't confident enough to present themselves to you. That would allow you, the consummate actor, to fully explore how it would feel to be alone, or to be with others but not gain satisfaction from the relationships.

So, you share this premise with your fellow actors, they agree to accept your premise, and you begin, developing the dialog and appropriate action as you go.

I invite you to stand in this idea, that you are the actor and that your 'character,' the role you play in the world, is being dreamed up by you. This is another world view, an alternate explanation, that we could entertain about our lives. Now, it's not easy to explore this story because it's completely at odds with common sense, with 'what everybody knows.' Exploring it requires momentarily disabling the filter of common sense.

Most of us have never explored the possibility that we might actually be dreaming, that this 'real' world might actually be a 'virtual' reality. But it is possible to go through your daily life looking at your experiences and your thoughts through the view that while *you* are real, your character, your personality, the 'I' which is reacting to all the situations you encounter, is made up … by you!

That view changes everything, everything about your life, your hopes and dreams, and your expectations. It offers you a wholly different idea of possibility and of freedom. It's like watching a drama about the challenges and difficulties of living, watching the expressions and body language of these impeccable actors on stage as they express these difficulties and their agonies, and then seeing their smiling faces when they take their curtain calls. Imagine those actors who awaken from immersion in their roles, their characters, to soak in the appreciation of the audience and the satisfaction of an acting job well done. Imagine one of them as ... your Self!

Much like actors who take on various roles, sometimes heroes, sometimes villains, we grow in wisdom and maturity the more roles we take on, in our repeated visits to planet Earth. Our roles on the planet certainly differ in content. They differ in time and in geographic locale, and they differ in terms of the symbols of affluence or lack thereof. So do the characters on the stage at your local playhouse. However, when it comes time for the curtain call, they all smile and take in the audience's gratitude for a great performance. And they are all equal.

And it MAY be, that in our greater role as serial actors, that which clouds or colors our joy and satisfaction, that which calls forth unhappiness and dissatisfaction, all that will turn out to be ... only a bunch of superstitions!

Getting to 'yes'

If we knew in our hearts that each and every experience is offered to us by an all-knowing, loving consciousness that wants only that we be happy and fulfilled, how would we behave? I believe we would say yes to everything! However, humans on the planet in this age are typically not firm in our knowledge of that universal loving awareness.

In my experience, learning to say yes has involved making a further distinction: there is a difference between saying yes with the Ego and saying yes with the Self. I believe there is only one way to fully make that distinction, and that is to experience both. What follows is are a couple of examples offered in illustration of saying yes with the Ego versus saying yes with the Self.

I spent my childhood saying yes to my parents. As a small child I understood, without ever being told, that my parents' role in this life was to give the gift of classical music to innumerable audiences and colleagues. My role, accordingly, was to be presentable, well-behaved, and quiet. In this manner I made my parents both available to their audiences and proud of me. As I came to see it, I earned their love and attention, expending untold quantities of boyish energy trying to please them. I was saying yes with my Ego and suppressing my Self in the process.

Studying physics in college and graduate school, I was seeking an understanding of how the world, and life, actually work. My studies led to mastery of the topics and proficiency with the mathematics but never the depth of understanding I wanted to have. I was saying yes to an obvious and predictable career path but doing so in an effort to be responsible and to act in accordance with my picture of the way an adult in my position should act. With slowly dwindling enthusiasm, I was saying yes with my Ego, and finding it ultimately unsatisfying.

After my academic career abruptly ended, and after an interlude being politically active in trying to stop the Vietnam War, I found I had reached the end of my desire to plan what to do with my life. So I moved to Aspen, Colorado, in 1970 with nothing but an invitation from an old friend to play folk music in clubs. I said yes with my Self to that invitation, and to the numerous musical invitations that followed.

Saying a heartfelt "yes" many times over during the next eight years, I had the opportunity to tour nationally as a musician with John Denver during the high point of his career. I toured the West Coast with Steve Martin as a member of his opening act, appeared on several national television shows, and literally had the time of my life to that point. That period in my life was truly magical and completely unplanned.[11]

In reviewing my life thus far, my awareness of the difference between saying yes with the Ego and saying yes with the Self is both profound and unmistakable. It wasn't until I discovered the seer's explanation that I could place those experiences in an appropriate context. Those opportunities were not just lucky, or extremely fortuitous. In the context of the seer's explanation, wherein *the fulfillment of the heart's desire is limited only by one's resistance to it*, those experiences were confirmation of the truth of who we really are. This lifetime has above all taught me the impact of the words of Juan Matus:

> For me there is only the traveling on the paths that have heart, on any path that may have a heart. There I travel, and the only worthwhile challenge for me is to travel its full length. And there I travel—looking, looking, breathlessly.[12]

---

[11] If you're interested in 'the rest of the story,' to quote Paul Harvey, it's on my website at https://www.larrygottlieb.com

[12] Carlos Castaneda, *The Teachings of Don Juan: A Yaqui Way of Knowledge*, (New York: Simon and Schuster, 1973), 11.

The end

Actually, there is no end! I am always available (and eager) to hear from you to further this conversation. You can reach me at:

www.LarryGottlieb.com

ACKNOWLEDGMENTS

In addition to those primary teachers to whom I refer in the text, Carlos Castaneda, Werner Erhard, Prem Rawat, and Esther Hicks, I want to thank several friends whose input has been indispensable in this effort.

My undying thanks go to Kay Knickerbocker, my wife, partner, and best friend, who edited this manuscript multiple times and whose support was critical to bringing this project to a successful conclusion.

Nancy Langer read the manuscript and offered valuable suggestions. Others with whom I discussed these ideas to my great benefit include Luke Gottlieb, Golden Sha, Jeanné Soulsby, Jan Garrett, Charles Savaiano, John Field, Charles Morris, Jan Diepersloot, Barry Schwartz, Bobby Mason, JD Martin, and all the folks at A Spiritual Center in Carbondale, Colorado. My 'head shot' is by Luke Gottlieb. Illustration work is by Kearby Milliner, Rachel Becker, and Nancy Sloan.

ABOUT THE AUTHOR

Larry Gottlieb earned his degrees in physics from MIT and the University of California. He has always wanted to know how the world works and felt physics would answer his questions in a definitive way. However, one day a life-changing experience could not be explained in that context, and he suddenly realized there was more to this inquiry than he could have imagined.

Over the last 45 years, Larry has endeavored to explain what happened that day and this has led him to a larger understanding of what it means to be a human being.

He has lectured, led discussions and workshops, written blogs, and recorded podcasts that captures this unique way of observing the world and its inhabitants.

Living in Colorado with his wife, Larry continues this inquiry in writings and conversations. He can be reached at larry@larrygottlieb.com.